Donald D. Green
4801 S Milnor Dr.
Memphis, TN 38128

3⁰⁰

W9-BUI-205

Advance Praise for
The Courage to Laugh

"This is a book that is not just about humor but life."

—BERNIE SIEGEL, M.D., author of *Love, Medicine, and Miracles*

"Allen Klein is a gem. His humor is not just a tickling of the mind, but a touching of the heart."

—STEPHEN LEVINE, author of *Who Dies?*

"When human tragedy becomes overwhelming, humor becomes the all-natural do-it-yourself wonder drug. *The Courage to Laugh* is a must-read therapy that encourages you to weep when you must and chuckle when you can."

—RABBI EARL A. GROLLMAN, D.D., author of
Living When a Loved One Has Died

"*The Courage to Laugh* is the glue that binds mind, body, and soul when we need it most—a survival manual that you cannot live without."

—BARRY BITTMAN, M.D., neurologist, CEO TouchStar Productions

"A great resource for caregivers. *The Courage to Laugh* will tickle your imagination and help you find hope and courage in the funniest places."

—DALE LARSON, PH.D., author of *The Helper's Journey*

"Never has the transcendent potential of humor been more clearly illuminated."

—CLIFFORD KUHN, M.D., University of Louisville Medical School

"At last a book to help midwife death, help make it fun. Think of the options."

—PATCH ADAMS, M.D.

Praise for *The Healing Power of Humor*

"Provides practical advice as to the fundamental importance of humor and laughter."

—STEVE ALLEN

"A must gift for anyone in the hospital, sick bed, or just feeling blue."

—HAROLD BLOOMFIELD, M.D., author of *Making Peace with Yourself*

"Two smiles up! 'Jollytologist' Allen Klein has written a wonderful book."

—*Hospice* magazine

"Written by a man who knows the pain of loss, this rare book reflects sensitivity, understanding, and a wonderful sense of humor."

—S.F., Ann Arbor

"When I heard myself laugh after reading your book, I realized I was on my way to recovery."

—M.O., Albuquerque

The
Courage
to
Laugh

Humor, Hope,

and Healing

in the Face

of Death

and Dying

The
Courage
to
Laugh

Allen Klein

Jeremy P. Tarcher / Putnam
a member of
Penguin Putnam Inc.
New York

Most Tarcher/Putnam books are available at special quantity discounts for bulk purchases for sales promotions, premiums, fund-raising, and educational needs. Special books or book excerpts also can be created to fit specific needs. For details, write Putnam Special Markets, 375 Hudson Street, New York, NY 10014.

Jeremy P. Tarcher/Putnam
a member of
Penguin Putnam Inc.
375 Hudson Street
New York, NY 10014
http://www.penguinputnam.com

Copyright © 1998 by Allen Klein
All rights reserved. This book, or parts thereof, may not
be reproduced in any form without permission.
Published simultaneously in Canada

Library of Congress Cataloging-in-Publication Data

Klein, Allen.
    The courage to laugh : humor, hope, and healing
in the face of death and dying / Allen Klein.
        p.   cm.
    Includes bibliographical references.
    ISBN 0-87477-929-4 (alk. paper)
    1. Terminally ill—Religious life. 2. Death—Religious aspects.
3. Wit and humor—Religious aspects. I. Title.
BL625.9.S53K54   1998   98-14923 CIP
291.4'42—dc21

Printed in the United States of America

10   9   8   7   6   5   4   3   2   1

This book is printed on acid-free paper. ♾

Book design by JUDITH STAGNITTO ABBATE

Acknowledgments

THE idea for this book occurred to me well over ten years ago. To thank all of those who have contributed to this project over that time span would probably take many pages, if I could even remember most of their names.

So instead I want to thank those who immediately come to mind: My literary agent, Shelley Roth, who helped this book come to fruition. My editor, David Groff, whose keen eye advised what to keep and what to cut. My writers' group and my colleagues from the National Speakers Association. Lauren Barnert, for her ongoing assistance. Alice Potter and Dave Cooperberg, for diligently proofing the manuscript. The San Francisco Public Library system, for their invaluable research assistance. And all the courageous people who shared their wonderful and often witty personal stories with me.

Perhaps the person who unknowingly contributed most to this book is not a person at all. It is my dog, Josh. I have learned a lot from Josh, including unconditional love, staying in the present, and going with the flow. But most of all, I acknowledge Josh as a major contributor because it was on our morning walks together that I first got, and then clarified, many ideas in this book. Thanks, Josh!

To my friends and acquaintances who, because of AIDS, are here only in spirit:

Andy Z., Bill N., Dennis G., Duncan C., Fred W., Gary W., George G., Glenn J., Guy C., Jack L., Jeffrey N., Jim F., Joe Z., John A. and John S., Joseph D., Kent S., Lalit D., Leon M., Lin C., Lloyd E., Mark F., Michael A. and Michael T., Paul H., Peter A. and Peter M., Randy H. and Randy S., Richard B., Rick S., Roger G., Sam A., Sandy C., Stephen M., Steve A., Tim S., and Tom W.

Contents

First Words   *xv*

Part I: Is Death Too Serious for Humor?   *1*

Chapter 1 • Humor and Death: "Tasteless" or "Triumphant"?   *3*
  The Courage to Laugh   *3*
  In the Face of Death   *5*
  Death's Paradox   *7*
  Tasteless? Triumphant?   *8*

Chapter 2 • Humor: Hope and Healing   *13*
  Humor and Hope   *13*
  Humor and Healing   *15*
    Coping   *15*
    Communicating   *20*
    Connecting   *21*

Chapter 3 • Humor: Uses and Abuses   *25*
  That Laughing Place   *25*
  Helpful Humor   *26*
  Hurtful Humor   *32*

Chapter 4 • Lessons in Laughter   36
    Comedians Laugh at Death   36
    Cartoonists Laugh at Death   39
    Hollywood Laughs at Death   41
    Television Laughs at Death   42
    Clowns Laugh at Death   47

Part II: Seeing Demise Thru Humorous Eyes   53

Chapter 5 • What's So Funny About HAspitals?   55
    The Bizarreness of It All   55
    A Certain Shocking Audacity   57

Chapter 6 • Hospice: Serious? Yes. Solemn? No Way! 67
    Humor and the Hospice Patient   67
    Humor and the Hospice Staff   74

Chapter 7 • The C-Words: Cancer and Comedy   81
    Putting Cancer in the Background   81
    The Comedic Accoutrements of Cancer   85
    Finding Joy   90
    Creatively Conquering Cancer   93

Chapter 8 • AIDS Ain't Funny—or Is It?   102
    All Its Garish Colors   102
    Something to Laugh About   103
    Can't Afford Not To   119

Chapter 9 • Kids: Great Wisdom from Small Fry   121
    You've Got to Be "Kidding"   121
    Turning Tears to Laughter   123

Chapter 10 • Lingering Loss   135
    Humor and Loss of Self   135
    Humor and Loss of Independence   142
    Humor and Loss of Freedom   147

Chapter 11 • Sudden Loss   155
    Humor and Fatal Accidents   155
    Humor and Suicide   157
    Humor and Disasters   159

Part III: Leave 'Em Laughing   165

Chapter 12 • Last Laughs   167
    Last Wishes   167
    Last Words   171
    Last Writes   173

Chapter 13 • Celebration of Loss   179
    Funeral Arrangements   180
    Memorable Memorials   183
    Humorous Eulogies   187

Chapter 14 • Mirth and Mourning   192
    Grief Relief   192
    Mirthful Memories   199

Final Words   205

Permissions   207
Bibliography   209

First Words

Sometimes a laugh is the only weapon we have.
—ROGER RABBIT

WHILE I was writing this book, my dad died. New Year's Eve 1996, he was taken to the hospital. Nine days later, just hours after my mom called to tell me that he was looking better, my dad was no longer alive. After a frantic phone call to book a flight and only two hours of sleep, I got on a plane that took me from my California home to my mom's condo in Florida and to the funeral.

I managed to hold back my tears until I was on the plane. There, however, amid businessmen using telephones and the click of laptops, I sat sobbing.

So here I was, I thought, writing about humor and death while my dad died. The universe was testing me to see if I could find anything funny in the situation—and I was failing. I found nothing to laugh about as the shock of his death washed over me. Nothing funny, that is, until the flight attendant shoved a cup of hot liquid under my nose and demanded, "Here. Drink this. I guarantee it will help."

"What is it?" I asked.

"Coffee and Bailey's Irish Cream," he said.

That's when my tears mingled with laughter. First of all, it was seven o'clock in the morning—not exactly cocktail hour. Second, I laughed because I never drink coffee and, since I am lactose intolerant, I avoid dairy products—especially cream.

I refused the attendant's grief-relief remedy, but there was something special about it anyway. The comic irony of it all made me laugh—not a laugh big enough to completely stop the tears, but an inner laugh that felt comfortable and whispered that everything would be all right.

Then I had another cosmic chuckle. I realized that I was just handed the opening words for this book.

During the next few days, I cried a lot. I was feeling alone and very vulnerable. My mother kept saying not to cry, but I allowed my tears to flow. I also noticed that in spite of the sadness of the situation, amusing incidents happened anyway. These drew me away from my tears and produced everything from a smile to a hearty guffaw.

One laugh came as a result of a watchman who would not allow my brother to enter my parents' condo. My mom had told the people at the front gate that she would be having lots of visitors in the next couple of days. She gave them her last name and asked them to put it on the guest list. When my brother tried to get in, they stopped him. "Klein," they said, was not on the list. When he informed them that his father had just died, they said, "Oh, in that case it's okay. You're on the *Death List!*"

Of course they had a Death List. This was, after all, a senior community. They had one all the time. But how was he supposed to know whether he needed to ask them to look on the *Death List* or on the *Not-Yet-Dead List?*

The next laugh, and this was a big one, came as we were having a telephone conversation with the rabbi. In the Jewish religion, it is customary for the immediate family to sit shivah for seven days after the funeral. Friends, relatives, and neighbors stop by to pay their condolences during this time. While informing the rabbi that my brother would be completing his shivah in Connecticut, where he lives, my mom had a slip of the tongue. Instead of saying, "Sitting shivah," she blurted out, "Shitting sivah."

My brother and I immediately convulsed with laughter. My mom, realizing what she had said, shoved the phone into my hand. She was laughing too hard to speak.

For the next few days, as I was going through this roller-coaster ride of tears and laughter, I learned several things about humor and grief.

I learned that it may take some time to find laughter after a loss. I learned too that it may not always be the fall-down-and-hold-your-belly kind of laughter that we had experienced when my mom got tongue-tied. Sometimes it's only an inner chuckle. But whatever kind it is, it is there. It is there to provide a momentary respite from our grief. It is there to show us that, indeed, life goes on in spite of our loss. It is there to give us hope.

If you have lost someone dear to you recently, I will not tell you to read this book because—as the flight attendant told me—"I guarantee it will help." No one can guarantee an instant grief remedy; I don't think there is one. What I can say from my own experience, however, is that humor might help. Maybe it will give you hope to continue and a much needed respite from your tears.

When a family is sitting shivah, it is customary for condolence callers to bring food into the home so that the bereaved do not have to cook or prepare meals. While callers are there, remembrances of the deceased are frequently discussed. Often they encompass some lighthearted moments in the deceased's life. Like the food that the condolence callers bring to provide nourishment for the body, I believe, the things they laugh about provide nourishment for the soul.

Seven days after my dad died, newspaper headlines reported that comedian Bill Cosby's only son was shot and killed. My dad had lived a full life; he was two weeks shy of his eighty-sixth birthday. Cosby's son, Ennis, was gunned down at age twenty-seven. Still, Cosby showed the world that life and laughter go on. Just days after his son died, he resumed taping his TV show and did two live performances in Florida, not too far from where my dad had lived. Onstage, with laughter and tears, he shared details of his son's funeral.

While many thought that Cosby had returned to work too soon, he obviously felt otherwise. In his grief, one of America's top-paid entertainers and most talented comedians said, "It's time for me to tell the people that we have to laugh—we've got to laugh."

Part I

Is Death

Too Serious

for

Humor?

Chapter 1

Humor and Death: "Tasteless" or "Triumphant"?

> I have always set personal boundaries of what is funny and what is not. I have been quoted as saying, "There are just some things you don't poke fun at." I was wrong. Laughter rises out of tragedy when you need it the most and rewards you for your courage.
>
> —ERMA BOMBECK

The Courage to Laugh

I call myself a *jollytologist*. I go around the country presenting speeches and seminars on humor. This unusual career began shortly after my wife died, from primary biliary cirrhosis—a rare liver disease. I started to explore the value of humor because of the important role it had played before, during, and after her death.

At first it seemed strange to me that my career in humor would emerge out of a loss. But as I began to work in the death-and-dying field, it seemed less bizarre. I found others who had followed a similar path.

For example, a popular corporate trainer of humor-in-business programs discovered the coping value of humor when he worked with terminally ill children. The founder of a national humor organization learned about the anxiety-relieving attributes of humor from a joking taxicab driver who sped his ill father to the hospital. And a friend and colleague of mine found that presenting humor workshops helped him heal his grief when his wife, like mine, passed away.

After investigating humor's benefits for approximately a dozen years now and frequently seeing how humor uplifts people's spirits during a loss, I am no longer surprised by the connection between humor and death.

Certainly illnesses such as cancer or AIDS may not be what we think of as laughing matters. After all, they often involve pain and the loss of life or limb. Still, life goes on and funny things happen in spite of illness and death.

Anyone who has worked in the death-and-dying arena knows, for example, that humor will frequently rear its head during the strangest of times. It is nature's way of giving us a perspective on a situation and allowing us to rise above it. Humor helps us keep our balance when life throws us a curveball.

I am *not* advocating that humor should cover up grief or that laughter need replace tears. It is important to grieve the loss of a loved one. Unresolved grief often causes problems down the road.

What I am saying is that laughter and tears are both valid in the dying and grieving process. Often, however, our attitude toward death is one of strict seriousness. Humor and death are frequently considered to be at opposite ends of the spectrum. Many people feel that laughing about anything dealing with death goes beyond the bounds of good taste.

My literary agent, for example, submitted the proposal for this book to a number of publishers. It drew strong reactions. Editors' comments, because of the juxtaposition of humor and death, ran from high praise to downright disapproval.

On the positive side, one editor said that the book had "a heartwarming message to convey." On the negative side, another editor wrote that the proposal was "right on the edge of being tasteless." Naturally, I was delighted with the first reaction, but it was the latter response that really surprised me.

You see, I thought that just because a situation is serious, it need not be solemn.

I thought that life, as George Bernard Shaw said, "does not cease to be funny when people die any more than it ceases to be serious when people laugh."

I thought that as Katharine Hepburn once stated, "we're finally at a point where we've learned to see death with a sense of humor."

But not everyone agrees. Christina Middlebrook, for example, a woman facing cancer, writes that "dying is difficult enough without having to achieve a pleasant attitude in the process." In her book *Seeing the Crab,* Middlebrook discusses historical references to death as a festive or joyous event; still, she feels that it "demeans death's power to whitewash it with the words *festive* or *joyous.*"

Certainly I am not the one to tell someone with terminal cancer that joy can be found there, or to tell the person with AIDS who informed me, "There is nothing funny about this disease," that there is.

What I do know, however, is that humor helped me get through several losses in my life and, as you will see in the numerous heartwarming and often hilarious stories in this book, that it helped others, too, to bear the unbearable. I share their stories here in hopes that both you and I can learn from these courageous people.

....

A sense of humor can help you overlook the unattractive, tolerate the unpleasant, cope with the unexpected, and smile through the unbearable.

—MOSHE WALDOKS

....

In the Face of Death

In my first book, *The Healing Power of Humor,* I wrote about the humor I found during my wife's terminal illness. I continue to share that story with my audiences nationwide, and for those not familiar with it, reprint it here.

Years ago, my wife, Ellen, lay dying in the hospital, a copy of Playgirl by her side. Suddenly, she opened to the male nude centerfold and insisted it be put on the wall.

"I think it's too risqué for the hospital," I said.

"Nonsense," she replied. "Just take a leaf from the plant over there and cover up the genitals."

I did as she requested. This worked well for the first day. Everything was okay for the second day. By the third day, however, the leaf started to shrivel up and reveal more and more of what we were trying to conceal.

We laughed every time we looked at a plant or a dried-up leaf. The duration of our levity may have lasted only ten or twenty seconds, but it brought us closer together, revived us, and steered us through our sea of darkness.

I again experienced humor's healing power when my father-in-law was near death, several years ago. He had just come home from one of his hospital stays. It was also his and my mother-in-law's wedding anniversary, so I suggested that they invite a few friends over for dinner and I would make a turkey.

Jimmy managed to get out of bed to join us. He enjoyed the meal, but the strain of feeding himself and the presence of guests were obviously tiring him. Noticing this, and knowing that he could not hear very well, my mother-in-law wrote a note and passed it to me to give to him. I read it and got hysterical with laughter. She remembered what she just wrote and laughed out loud too.

The note said, "Happy Anniversary, dear. Do you want to go to bed?"

Jimmy read what his wife had written, looked up across the table, and with a twinkle in his eye and a smile on his face, he said to her, "I would love to, dear, but we have company."

I shared this story at Jimmy's memorial service and realized afterward that the laughter helped balance the pain and provided us with a fond memory of his final hours.

Laughter also played an important role in another incident. I recall how my friend Rick comforted me with humor when he was dying of AIDS. I once went into Rick's house, and there on the wall was a Star of David, a picture of the Buddha, and a crucifix—and Rick was a Quaker!

I said, "Rick, how come you have all of these diverse religious symbols?"

He said, "You never know who's right. I'm covering all my bases."

I'm convinced Rick lived so long with AIDS because of his sense of humor. He was able to joke about himself and his illness.

Every year Rick would have a birthday party, and every year he would poke fun of the fact that he was still alive. One year his invitation read: "RICK'S FOURTH ANNUAL LAST BIRTHDAY PARTY. He Lived Through Another Year, Can You Believe It?"

Even his obituary, which I'm sure he had a hand in writing, was poignantly funny. It read:

Rick Saporito
February 16, 1948—June 19, 1992
Quaker
Marine
Housewife

I have found humor in the midst of death in my professional life as well. When I was a volunteer with hospice, one patient, who was very near death, refused to eat. She said, "Why should I eat? I'm going to die soon anyway."

The following day, she again announced her intention not to eat. By the third day, however, she arose from her bed and joined her family at the breakfast table. The amazed family members wanted to know how come she was joining them for breakfast after so many days of not eating.

The frail, elderly lady turned and said, "So who wants to die on an empty stomach?"

Another time, one of my hospice patients proclaimed that after she died, she wanted her ashes put in some paint and the bedroom repainted.

When I said that I was puzzled at her request, she replied that it made perfect sense: "Then I can look down from the ceiling and see if there is any hanky-panky going on."

Even today I continue to find people with life-challenging issues who value humor. For example, there are hundreds of messages posted on one computer bulletin board entitled "The Lighter Side of HIV." Why this interest in humor from people whose life may be limited? Because, proclaims the bulletin board's opening message, "Despite the seriousness of HIV, many of us have found that sharing a sense of humor about it can help immensely."

....

Here is the paradox: although cancer was the worst thing that ever happened to me, it was also the best. Cancer . . . enriched my life, made me wiser, made me happier. Another paradox: although I would do everything possible to avoid getting cancer again, I am glad I had it.

—BETTY ROLLIN, *First, You Cry*
....

Death's Paradox

There is another area of death and dying related to humor. It can be found in the paradoxes surrounding life's final moments.

Perhaps the most prominent death-related paradox is the bittersweet quality of death itself. On the one hand, the loss of a loved one is harsh. But on the other hand, there is some sweetness in knowing that death can put an end to a loved one's suffering.

I have always been attracted to bittersweet things. Perhaps that is, in part, the reason for my attraction to death and humor. I see death not as a sorrowful termination of a lifetime, but as the culmination of one's existence and the beginning of another—a death and a birth all at once. All the joy of birth and all the sorrow of death are brought into one bittersweet moment.

In our culture, we have chosen to emphasize the loss of everything and the *difference* between life and death. In ancient Eastern cultures, life and death are not classified as opposing forces but simply as aspects of existence. Perhaps these Eastern cultures are more attuned to the paradoxical, bittersweet nature of death.

Another paradox is the fact that we seem to be both repelled and intrigued by death at the same time. We ship our deceased off to a mortuary for rituals that once were performed at home, yet we are constantly bringing reminders of death into our house through grim media headlines and gruesome television shows.

Several other paradoxes also exist. Many people, for example, use the words *frightening, painful,* or *horrible* when they think of death. But at the same time others find *peace, release,* and *triumph* more appropriate.

After my wife, Ellen, died, I found some of her writing. One place was especially poignant. It talked about loving life and not wanting to leave, but the next sentence spoke of Ellen's paradox. She always loved mysteries. In fact, when she died, I found 110 murder mysteries in our library. Ellen's paradox was that although she loved life, dying would solve life's greatest mystery: "The hereafter holds a great temptation out to me," she wrote. "I love mysteries, and having the answer to that one would be gratifying. But I do love life. The choice continues to boggle my mind and my reason. I know too that I love drama, and perhaps this is all merely part of the big show."

There may be humor on the way to the gallows, but not in the hanging itself.

—ARNOLD BEISSER, M.D., *Flying Without Wings*

Tasteless? Triumphant?

While I was doing research for this book, I came across a dialogue on the Internet about humor and death. It was started by a nurse who was seeking "humorous personal-experience stories about the end of life." Her simple request touched off a debate on both sides of the issue. Here, beginning with the irate reply, I present the gist of the on-line conversation:

It is obvious that you have not experienced the death of a loved one. There is simply nothing humorous about death to those that are most affected by it. Death is part of life, we will all die, some too soon and some after much suffering. . . . It happens to some without warning, to some after a long battle with illness. Some people die alone, unnoticed. The lucky ones die with their loved ones. . . . This can never be humorous. . . . Never funny.

Consider that some nurses, paramedics, doctors, etc., see death every day. . . . You're right—it's never funny. But put yourself in their shoes—they have to keep working—they have to avoid going insane—they have to come to work tomorrow—and above all, they have to do their job to keep the next patient from suffering the same fate. How do you deal with this? . . . Everyone finds a different way, and for many it's humor.

It truly surprises me how many people have posted here who are so uncomfortable with the subject of death that they cannot see room for humor. . . . Those who deal with death routinely understand. But those who deal with it only as a personal tragedy don't understand, and probably never will.

So many of us seem incapable of dealing with even the concept of death with any reaction other than horror. There is something I read, once, from a man in Spain who was talking of women, bullfighting and death. He said that by giving birth to a child only women can create something new, thus overcoming death. This man went on to tell of how men have no way to confront death. All they can do, like the bullfighter facing the bull, is taunt it, spit at it. Man can only overcome death, in a similar way, by laughing at it, by taunting it.

I have experienced the deaths of several loved ones. I still find humor in death. I hope when I die that people will be sad to see me go but can laugh and smile at the memories of happy times and funny episodes.

I'm an emergency room nurse. . . . There is often humor in death . . . it is the only way to cope with the sadness I see at work every day. I also lost my father six years ago, and my eighteen-year-old niece just last May, and I can tell you there was much humor in both their deaths. We laughed with my father up until the end; in fact, he died with the sound of my mother's and my laughter still ringing in his ears. . . . Knowing my father, he would have been angry had we *not* laughed.

Next time you're faced with having to deal with someone's death, look for the humor—you might be surprised at how it lightens the load. In my family, we laugh, joke and tell the funniest stories about the deceased that we've ever heard. Yes, we also cry and certainly we mourn, but the humor is what gets us through the day.

In reading these postings, I realized that they touched on several important points—most of which will be expanded upon later in this book. They are

- Death itself is not funny. Things that happen around it are.
- Our only real weapon against death is humor.
- Those who work in the death-and-dying arena understand the need for humor; those who do not, may not.
- Some people will never see the humor/death connection.
- Most people don't want survivors to be morose after they die.
- You can laugh and cry at a loss. Both are appropriate.
- No matter how serious a situation is, humor can help us get through the day.

I agree that there is nothing funny about death itself. But as you will see throughout this book, there is humor on the way to death as well as afterward. There is humor in terminal illness and in grief. There is humor surrounding sudden death and lingering loss.

There is even humor in our attempts to avoid the mention of death. Frequently these euphemistic substitutes for death are ridiculously funny. For example:

met his end (Was the deceased double-jointed?)
her clock has run down (Where are those Eveready batteries when we need 'em?)
called home (ET, where are you?)
answered the call of the unknown (Salespeople phoning again?)

called beyond (I hope they used the discounted evening rates.)
bit the dust (What, no vacuum cleaner?)

In *The Last Dance*, authors Lynne Ann DeSpelder and Albert Lee Strickland write about a humorous euphemistic death story:

> Doctors at a teaching hospital avoided using the word "death" when a patient died because of their concern that other patients might become alarmed. One day, as a medical team was examining a patient, an intern came to the door with information about the death of a patient. Knowing that the word "death" was taboo and finding no ready substitute, she stood in the doorway and announced, "Guess who's not going to shop at Woolworth's any more."

[handwritten margin notes: Never say crash to a pilot / Time at small age ask, what do you do when the plane crashes / Ans never you never say crash to a pilot]

Finally, there is even humor in no death. Consider, for example, the ludicrousness of living forever. Would you get anything done? Why try? You have forever! And if there were no death, what about the absurdity of trying to provide food and housing for an ever-expanding population that never dies?

Death is an important and needed element of our life cycle. We may not like it, but that's the way it is. And the more we deny it—the more we push it away—the unhappier we become.

I am not advocating that we go around singing death's praises. But seeking the laughter among the tears can help us balance death's inevitability.

> If the question of comedy is the question of how to live with incongruity, then, since death is the final incongruity, the ultimate question of comedy is the question of death.
>
> —A. ROY ECKARDT, *On the Way to Death*

So, in death-and-dying situations, is humor "tasteless," or "triumphant"?

Please, don't answer that just yet.

First read the story about how humor helped a woman whose husband died in a plane crash get on with her life, or the story of how humor helped prisoners interned in concentration camps survive, or how it helped people put their lives back together after a major disaster, or . . .

The stories in this book are not fiction. I did not make them up. They originate from people who found humor in their darkest times. For them, humor amid death was not tasteless; it was triumphant. It was their tool, and sometimes their only tool, for hope, healing, and sometimes survival.

The stories in this book are meant to do three things. First, they document the presence of humor in death-and-dying situations. Second (I hope, dear reader) they will lift your spirit with laughter. And third, they show that if others can find something to laugh about in their bleakest moments, then perhaps you can too.

Chapter 2

Humor:
Hope and Healing

Tragedy gives us a sense of human courage, comedy a sense
of wild irrational hope.
                    —PETER BERGER, *The Precarious Vision*

Humor and Hope

There were three hundred people in the room, but she stood out immediately. While others were chatting away, she sat alone in silence. While others were interacting, she sat staring into nothingness and bent over as if pressed down by some great weight.

I lost track of this woman while presenting my humor program, but when it was over she came up to the front of the room to speak to me. "I haven't laughed in almost two years—not since my young son was killed in an auto accident," she said. "Your program showed me that I can go on with my life. I can live again. I can laugh again." She thanked me and left quickly.

In addition to comments such as this, I also get unsolicited letters from time to time. I don't know the people who write these notes, but they know me because my first book touched them in some way. One such letter came from a woman in Albuquerque, New Mexico.

Margaret was in a horrendous car crash that took the lives of her daughter and her cousin. The accident left her with an extreme head injury, which has taken years to heal.

In her letter to me, she wrote, "I first read *The Healing Power of Humor* about five years ago. I was lying behind a curtain in a physical therapy room. As I was reading, I laughed loudly over and over. The physical therapists looked around the curtain, wanting to get in on the joke. They didn't know it, but when I heard myself laugh, I realized I was on my way to recovery.

"The laughter," she said, "showed me that I was coming back to myself. I didn't realize how much laughter was missing until I heard myself. I hadn't laughed for so long."

While I was flattered by the comments of these women, I realized that I was only the conduit in helping them find the humor that surrounded them all along. I also realized that humor gave them hope.

Finding humor in a tragic situation is an extremely healthy step. It is a way of looking toward the future and of saying that this suffering can be put behind us. . . . Humor is something to strive for and to embrace. It is a way of saying, "The tragedy has *happened* to us, but it does not *define* us. Despite what we've been through, we are going ahead with our lives. . . . You didn't destroy us! We are still here. We are still laughing. And therefore we have life and hope."

—PETER WEINGOLD, M.D.

In exploring the relationship between hope and humor, I asked William Buchholz, M.D.—a northern California oncologist who writes about the element of hope in cancer patients—about their connection. He said, "Humor is like the seasoning that makes hope tasty. We can sustain ourselves with hope, but it's like a diet of bread and water, which can give us the ability to get up each day but not necessarily look forward to it. Humor adds the savoryness to the stew—the ability to enjoy the moment.

"Humor," Buchholz continued, "adds the extra element for the will to live that goes beyond hope and that actually is the thing that turns an experience from tolerable to desirable."

No matter what kind of life-challenging adversity people are facing, humor, like prayer, provides hope. In both laughter and prayer, we go beyond the world as we know it, transcending our predicament. We may not like the situation we are in, but whereas anger may draw us into our dilemma, a chuckle, like a prayer, can help us rise above it.

In the story below, the Reverend A. Stephen Pieters writes how humor gave him hope soon after he found out that he had a terminal illness:

The night in 1984 when they told me I had eight months to live,
I gathered friends around me and watched "I Love Lucy" re-runs.

We must have watched the "Vitameatavegamin" episode at least three times. Over and over, we played the part where Lucy gets drunk on the medicine, and we laughed more and more hysterically each time.

Laughing at Lucy was partially an escape from reality that night. She was a familiar, comfortable companion. Through her various TV shows, I had known her all my life. She was a safe haven of laughter at every point in my life when I felt vulnerable. And now, on that night of the most indescribable emotional pain, I derived a tremendous comfort from the familiar fun she presented with Ricky and Ethel and Fred.

And laughing that night also gave me my first taste of hope. The fact that I could feel such joy stated to me that life wasn't quite over, that joy was still possible, that life was still good.

Humor and Healing

If I were to simplify humor's role in death and dying, I would say that it not only gave people hope but in some way also helped them heal by providing a means of coping, communicating, and connecting. In this context, I am using the word *humor* in its broadest sense, as a metaphor for a full range of positive emotions. I am talking about hope, joy, pleasure, fun, happiness, celebration, optimism, and the will to live—all of which are important at a time when coping is overwhelming, communication often at a standstill, and connecting difficult.

Coping

> One of the most adaptive ways a human being has of dealing with severe illness and also with the finality of death itself is through humor.
> —RAYMOND MOODY, M.D.

Humor can alter any situation and help us cope at the very instant we are laughing. As one hospice worker I interviewed stated, "Humor has a force of its own. Like prayer, it transforms you."

In a study of well-known comedians, psychologist Samuel Janus found that nearly all of the laughmakers he investigated had experienced some major loss or suffering in their childhood. As a way of coping, they turned to humor to transform their pain.

Humor allows us to cope with both physical and mental pain in three ways:

- When we are dealing with death we are constantly being dragged down by the event. *Humor diverts our attention and lifts our sagging spirits.*
- Dealing with death is stressful. *Humor decreases our stress and tension.*
- In the midst of death, life feels out of balance. *Humor provides that balance by providing a fresh perspective and power in a powerless situation.*

Humor, like hope, allows one to acknowledge and endure what is otherwise unendurable.

—GAIL SHEEHY

Whether planned or not, laughter takes our mind off our troubles. It diverts our attention and gives us a break when things get too difficult. It distracts us and keeps us occupied so that time, if nothing else, can heal our wounds.

When we are in pain and wish that something would "take us away from all of this," humor does exactly that. It may be for only a brief moment of time, but humor distracts us from our pain, focuses our attention elsewhere, and lifts our sagging spirits.

Moreover, if we can be distracted for one moment, it is possible to extend that moment to the next, and to the one after that. I recall, for example, when I first started presenting all-day humor programs. One woman in the class had recently had an operation. She came to the workshop with both arms bandaged. Around eleven-thirty in the morning, the woman let out a shriek. I thought she was in pain, but she wasn't. She said, "I was enjoying myself and laughing so much since nine A.M. that I forgot to take my pain medication. For the first time since the operation, I haven't been in pain."

Why is it that at a wake the best laughter comes out? Because it's like a balloon—the greater the tension the tighter balloon.

—RICK SEGEL

Have you ever had a particularly bumpy airplane ride? And have you ever heard all the passengers applaud as the plane touched down? Humor is like that applause. In a tense situation, laughter, like the applause, provides the release of pent-up tension.

When Jeanne Harper, a counselor in private practice, was twenty-four, she needed a hysterectomy. The hospital had never done this surgery on someone so young before. Naturally, tension was high for both Harper and the operating room staff. So before they put her under sedation, Harper told the medical team, "You can take whatever you need to take out. I give you full permission. The only thing I ask is that you leave the 'playpen'."

The joke did exactly what Harper wanted it to do, which was to break the tension. "I couldn't be in control of what they found," she says, "but I could be in control of the atmosphere of the operating room."

> Humour, I think, is responsible for more important human advance than physics, medicine or any other science. It teaches us to see things in proportion.
>
> —GEORGE MIKES, *Humour in Memoriam*

One of the components of coping involves maintaining our balance. When we are dealing with the threat of death, life is out of balance. We lose our sense of humor and the equilibrium it can provide. When we add joy and humor back into it, life begins to upright itself again.

Humor gives us a distance from our problem and helps us keep our balance. It doesn't change our situation, but it does change how we view it. "Life," said Charlie Chaplin, "is a tragedy when seen in close-up but a comedy in longshot."

In the delightful book entitled *Crazy Wisdom,* author Wes "Scoop" Nisker playfully suggests that we reach for that comedy by viewing death differently:

> The very word "death" has become laden with negative connotations. Death. It sounds so sudden and final. Perhaps we should give it another name. This new name should refer to the transition of the spirit, the aura, the essence that we often call a person's "energy." Since we usually think of the spirit in terms of light, let's look at "light" as a metaphor. . . . Instead of calling this transformation death, we can now call it the "dissolve." It's still the big "D," but to dissolve implies only that one has lost one's outlines. We dissolve into that place where there is only darkness, or

into pure, eternal light. "We will all dissolve someday"; "She is sick and dissolving." After all, that is how we leave. We just fade from sight and from memory, and the show goes on.

During the dying process, perhaps more than at any other time in our life, we need to keep our perspective and our balance. Humor can help us do both of these instantly.

....

Humor is a rich and versatile source of power—a spiritual resource very like prayer which may be the best weapon to raise against the Angel of Death, who, like the devil, cannot bear to be mocked.

—MARILYN CHANDLER, "Healthy Irreverence"

....

Danny Williams is a nationally acclaimed gay comedian. In a newsletter published by Kairos, an organization that offers support for caregivers, Williams explained how humor was a means of self-defense and power for him:

> When I was a kid I had a condition where I wasn't producing gamma globulin and had to have frequent injections of it to preserve my immune system. I was always sick. I weighed nothing, because I had trouble keeping food down. I was so thin and looked so sickly that I was a prime target for getting beat up by other kids. I mean if you are going to beat up somebody you want to make sure they are smaller or weaker than you are . . . and I was this little "matchstick boy" who was a perfect target! The way I protected myself was to be funny. I would get people laughing and the big guys became protective of me because I was a funny guy.

Patients, families, and caregivers can take a lesson from Williams and other comedians who used humor for empowerment. Humor is a way of defending against any oppressor—whether it be another person, a serious illness, or even death.

For the survivor, humor can also be a source of strength and control. For example, one woman in her early twenties had her brother die when she was very young, her father die of cancer, and her mother die in a car crash. Yet in spite of all this loss, she says that "the more serious things are in my life, the more apt I am to come out of it with humor." She feels that humor acted as a booster. She says that the "situation still remained serious, but it was less taxing for me when I could laugh at it."

In his classic book in the humor field, *Laughter and Liberation,* Harvey Mindess sums up the power humor has over our oppressors, including such things as death, life-challenging illness, and loss. He says that "they may be more powerful than us, but our wit seeks out their defects so that, in laughing them down, we build ourselves up."

Freud felt that a high appreciation of death humor was a mark of maturity. He labeled this "gallows humor." It is the kind of humor that arises out of precarious and dangerous, life-threatening situations. Gallows humor is a way of laughing in the face of death, a way of overcoming our fear. A classic example of gallows humor was uttered by James Rodgers, a resourceful murderer who was executed by a rifle squad in 1960. When asked if he had a last request, he smilingly said: "Why yes, a bullet-proof vest."

Even if we are not facing the immediacy of the gallows, humor can help us get the upper hand on our death-related fears and anxieties. One therapist, for example, tells of a woman in her mid-thirties who was plagued by a fear of physical illness. "Despite her good health," the therapist said, "she reacted to any discomfort with fear and anticipation of a fatal disease." On one occasion the patient confided that she had always been afraid of dying young. To ease the patient's fears and help her see the absurdity of her actions, the therapist replied, "But it's too late—the most you can do is die middle-aged."

We feel helpless in the face of death, but when we can laugh about it, whether it be imminent or not, we begin to take control. We open the closet door and let some light in so that the bogeyman, that grim reaper, does not seem so frightening after all. Humor, as illustrated in the story below, empowers and gives an upper hand.

> Once a rabbi was giving a stirring sermon about the mortality of life and how everyone in his congregation would die one day. As he was speaking, the rabbi noticed a man grinning in the last row. After the service was over, the rabbi approached the man and asked, "Why, after I said that everyone in this congregation is going to die someday, did you smile like that?"
>
> The man responded, "I am not a member of this congregation! I am visiting from out of town."

Communicating

Can we talk?

—JOAN RIVERS

Humor not only enhances communication in serious situations but can also be a way of discussing taboo topics, of talking about death in a less threatening way and of opening doors to weighty matters.

During my wife's illness, I remember, we had a major argument. She wanted to go out dancing several nights a week, and I, per her doctor's orders, wanted her to stay in bed. She accused me of not supporting her aliveness and asked me to move out of the house for a while. It was a very painful and confusing time for both of us, but later I learned that each of us dies and grieves in a different way.

Ellen laughed, cried, and danced her way to the end. When medical advice was that she remain in bed, she danced until the disco clubs closed, and then went out for breakfast at three in the morning. When doctors advised lots of rest, Ellen would stay up all night. I realized, looking back, that for Ellen rest was for those who were sick. Bed was for sleeping and perhaps not waking up. If she kept dancing, perhaps she'd keep living.

Ellen's way of leaving this world certainly wasn't mine. My last breath would not be danced away. But Ellen's death was not mine. She died as she had lived. She whirled into people's lives, gave them some of her sparkle, and then vanished in an instant like the glitter from a fairy godmother's magic wand.

I share this story to illustrate how strained communication can be when someone is near death. I wish Ellen and I could have seen some humor in our differences at the time, as we had frequently done in other disagreements, but we did not.

On a more positive note, Kaye Ann Herth, a nurse and professor who has had extensive experience in working with terminally ill patients, found that she could use humor to open serious discussions. Herth says, "I began a visit with Ms. S., a young adult undergoing extensive radiation for Hodgkin's disease, by asking her how things were going. Although she said, 'Fine,' her nonverbal cues conveyed something else. I ventured, 'I bet you feel like a Crispy Critter.' She laughed, but then began to express her fears and concerns."

The following story, published in *Noetic Sciences Review* (autumn 1988) by Rachel Naomi Remen, M.D., also illustrates the power humor has to break down barriers and enhance communication.

> I had a man in my practice with osteogenic sarcoma of the leg, which was removed at the hip in order to save his life. He was 24 years old when I started working with him and he was a very angry man with a lot of bitterness, a deep sense of injustice and a very deep hatred for all the well people, because it seemed so unfair to him that he had suffered this terrible loss so early in life. After working with this man for a couple of years I saw a profound shift. He began "coming out of himself." He began visiting other people in the hospital who had suffered severe physical losses and he would tell me the most wonderful stories about these visits. Once he visited a young woman who was almost his own age. It was a hot day in Palo Alto and he was in running shorts so his artificial leg showed when he came into her hospital room. The woman was so depressed about the loss of both her breasts that she wouldn't even look at him, wouldn't pay any attention to him. The nurses had left her radio playing, probably in order to cheer her up. So, desperate to get her attention, he unstrapped his leg and began dancing around the room on one leg, snapping his fingers to the music. She looked at him in amazement, and then she burst out laughing and said, "Man, if you can dance, I can sing."

Connecting

> When a man is singing and cannot lift his voice, and another comes and sings with him, another who can lift his voice, the first will be able to lift his voice too. That is the secret of the bond between spirits.
>
> —HASIDIC SAYING

In an age where hospital patients are hooked up to a mountain of medical apparatus and human touch is minimal, humor can be a wonderful way of connecting. Lynn Erdman, an oncology nurse, says, "All people need the 'high touch' of laughter to help balance the 'high tech' treatment of cancer."

We often tend to forget that the seriously ill are more than just their illness. We allow their illness to monopolize everything else. Perhaps, unknowingly, we separate ourselves from them. We become "the well" and they become "the sick." A few chuckles shared between the terminally ill and another, however, bring those involved to equal territory—"If we can still laugh together, then I am no different from you."

In *When Your Loved One Is Dying,* Rabbi Earl Grollman, who has written so eloquently about the needs of the dying and the bereaved, writes:

> *Dying people need*
> *lightness and smiles in their lives.*
>
> *People who have a good sense of*
> *humor in their lifetimes often maintain their sense of humor*
> *in their dying.*
>
> *Somberness*
> *won't make you or your loved one better.*
>
> *A dying person quipped:*
> *"My situation is hopeless*
> *but not serious."*
>
> *Humor helped her manage feelings*
> *that were too great to deal with openly.*
>
> *The threat of her future*
> *was no less menacing,*
> *but it became a little easier to bear.*
>
> *Laughing together*
> *is one of the normal ways*
> *that people relate to each other.*
>
> *One patient said to a chaplain:*
> *"You've become so morbid and gloomy*
> *since you heard my prognosis.*
> *You used to tell me such humorous*
> *stories.*
> *I'm the same person that I was*
> *before the diagnosis.*
> *How come you aren't fun anymore?"*

We're not *fun* anymore because we often treat the terminally ill as if they are already dead.

Humor, on the other hand, emphasizes that the patient is still a living human being who can enjoy a moment of levity. As illustrated in the story below and again in the hospice chapter, laughter between the patient and someone else is saying, "I am not dead yet. I am still alive. We can still share something in common." In her book *It All Begins with Hope,* Ronna Fay Jevne aptly demonstrates this point:

> Leo was in the last stages of liver cancer. When he came to my office, he looked egg-yolk yellow. He reported that a hoped-for decision was not possible, that his ex-wife was already closing in for part of his estate, that his lawyer had said, "Don't worry, you're basically bankrupt," and that the pain was becoming intolerable. For some reason my spontaneous response was, "Other than that, how's your week been?" I was immediately concerned I had been inappropriate. However, Leo was laughing so hard I could hardly understand him as he said, "Thank goodness, someone still thinks I am alive! I am so tired of everyone treating everything so seriously."
>
> ....
> Laughter helps us remember all the things we have in common.
> —CLIFFORD KUHN, M.D.
> ....

For fourteen years, Barbara Adams Thompson was a hospice volunteer. During that time, she recorded stories about her dying patients and compiled them in her self-published book, *Sometimes We Laughed.* One of those people was a man with both AIDS and Parkinson's disease. He was not the easiest of patients to connect with, but it was humor, she says, that helped break down the barriers. Thompson writes:

> It's hard to say when our relationship began to change; perhaps it was when we began to laugh. I'm glad we got to laugh before it was time to cry. Once he told me that when he could not sleep, he got up and made a salad. "What kind did you make?" I asked. He looked at me, paused and with those arms and hands raised and flying, he said, "A tossed salad—what else could I do?" We laughed and I felt a door had opened. I was included in this circle of trusted friends.

Another woman, named Laura, had fourth-stage ovarian cancer. She talked about how an unexpected comic moment led to conversation and connecting:

> I worked hard over the oven and presented a tasty meal that everyone enjoyed. Just before dessert, I stepped into the bathroom, looked in the mirror and gasped! The entire front of my wig was a solid melted glob of plastic fibers. (Obviously, I had gotten too close to the oven when I was basting the bird.) What I couldn't believe was that NO ONE had said a word. They were trying to spare me the embarrassment.
>
> I walked back into the dining room laughing so hard at the thought of them all trying to ignore the hilarious sight of me in that wig. The laughter was contagious and before long everyone was in stitches. This laughter led us into the first heart to heart conversation we had had since my diagnosis. The tears shed in humor opened the doors to sharing the pain. The shields went down and hearts connected.

As you can see, healing is not just about curing. It is also about providing hope when life is challenged and, as the final story eloquently displays, helping hearts connect. Humor can do both.

Chapter 3

Humor:
Uses and Abuses

A good laugh and a long sleep are the two best cures.
—IRISH PROVERB

That Laughing Place

Just after my mother called to tell me about my dad's death, my brother tried to reach me, but I was on the phone booking my airline ticket. He got my answering machine, which, because of the humor workshops I present, starts off with lots of people laughing. When I finally spoke with my brother, he told me that listening to that laughter was painful.

I have always thought that if you approach humor with an open heart, there is no place where it is inappropriate. I was wrong. The death of my dad taught me that humor does not work when we are in a state of shock. Humor has to wait until after the shock has begun to subside. It has to be put on hold until after we experience, at least in some small way—as I did with the spiked-coffee-on-the-plane incident—that eventually everything will be all right.

Oliver Sacks, a neurological doctor and popular author, illustrates this point very well in his book *A Leg to Stand On*. An accident in which he is attacked by a bull on a desolate mountaintop in Norway renders him helpless—and humorless. It was not until the moment of his rescue, from what he thought would be his last day on earth, that he found any relief in laughter. Sacks writes:

I stammered out, in broken Norwegian, what had happened on the heights, and what I could not put into words I drew in the dust. . . . The two of them [his rescuers] laughed at my picture of the bull. They were full of humor, these two, and as they laughed I laughed too—and suddenly, with the laughter, the tragic tension exploded, and I felt vividly and, so to speak, comically alive once again. I thought I had had every emotion on the heights, but—it now occurred to me—I hadn't laughed once. Now I couldn't stop laughing—the laughter of relief, and the laughter of love, that deep-down laughter which comes from the center of one's being. The silence was exploded, that quite deathly silence which had seized me, as in a spell, those last minutes.

In this incident, Sacks illustrates an important point. Yes, laughter can release tension and provide relief, but frequently it doesn't happen until our shock wears off. Until that time, we can't really let go and laugh.

Once we arrive at that "laughing place," humor can be of great value in the death, dying, and grieving process.

Helpful Humor

> If grief deprives us of laughter, we are in trouble.
>
> —CLIFFORD KUHN, M.D.

HUMOR AND THE FIVE STAGES

In her best-selling book *On Death and Dying,* Elisabeth Kübler-Ross writes of the terminally ill encountering five stages—denial, anger, bargaining, depression, and acceptance. Humor can be a tool in helping the patient deal with these stages.

Denial humor, for example, can give the weary patient a much-needed reprieve. "Denial functions as a buffer," Kübler-Ross says; it "allows the patient to collect himself." Thus the sarcastic and cynical humor that many patients direct at their incapacities is part of an effort to gain a moment away from their pain and suffering.

Clifford Kuhn, a professor of psychiatry at the University of Louisville, in Kentucky, feels that there is a definite connection between humor and Kübler-Ross's five stages of dying. Kuhn says, "Denial can be funny." Denial, after all, is a kind of sticking your head in the sand—and he asks, "If your head is in the sand, what part of you is sticking up and very vulnerable?"

"What's funny about anger?" Kuhn asks. Then he points out that in times of anger, "we look more like a slapstick comedian than at any other time." When we get angry, Kuhn says, not only do we look stupid but we may say foolish things as well—"Oh yeah, oh yeah, oh yeah . . . Well, your mother is too."

Kuhn also asks, "Where is the humor in bargaining?" His answer compares bargaining in grief to haggling at a flea market. We bargain the salesperson down a few bucks but he has already inflated the price a few bucks, knowing we were going to bargain with him in the first place. "When we start bargaining in our grief," Kuhn says, "God must be at least as smart as a flea market merchant!"

Kuhn admits that the depression/sadness phase of grief may be the hardest in which to find something to laugh about. However, think of Charlie Chaplin and immediately you get to see how both sadness and laughter can coexist after all.

Humor also has a connection to acceptance, the final stage of grief. According to Kuhn, "Humor is a way of maintaining acceptance." He provides an example from his own life.

When Kuhn's first grandson, Jordan, was born prematurely, it was touch-and-go whether or not he would live. By the second day of the child's life, however, the family had accepted that the situation was under control. When Kuhn and his wife entered the hospital nursery, his wife noticed a blue light hanging above another child. Curious about it, she asked her doctor-husband why it was there. He spontaneously responded, "It's a bluelight special. That baby is on sale!"

That bit of humor, Kuhn says, helped them maintain their acceptance of the situation. "Grief brings us to acceptance. Laughter does that too."

When I could recognize something funny in what a moment before had seemed like a hopelessly grim situation, a wonderful transformation occurred. It was as though I had been suddenly healed and restored to health, even if only for a moment, and even if only in my mind.

—ARNOLD BEISSER, M.D., *Flying Without Wings*

How Would You Feel?

As she was discussing her dad's lung cancer, one woman told me, "We were too emotionally involved in what was happening to see the humor." Yet her father frequently joked about his illness and continued to do so until several weeks before his death.

What this woman shared is not surprising. Often, as we will see in the hospice chapter, it is patients who initiate the humor. They somehow intuitively know how much it helps them, and those around them, cope with their not-so-funny situations. Families and friends of the terminally ill frequently have a hard time understanding how a patient can do this. Perhaps the following story, told by Ram Dass in his book *Grist for the Mill*, will help them comprehend.

Ram Dass writes about a young mother of four who had been through eleven operations to rid her body of cancer. In a seminar she was attending on death and dying, the woman asked the audience, "How would you feel if you came into a hospital room to visit a twenty-eight-year-old mother dying of cancer?" The audience called out such answers as *angry, sad, full of pity, frustrated, confused, horror.* Then she asked, "How would you feel if you were that twenty-eight-year-old mother and everyone who came to visit felt those feelings?" Ram Dass goes on to say that "suddenly it was apparent to all of us how we surround such a being with our reactions to death."

While the patient may know the value of humor, family and friends might be reluctant to invite humor into the situation. The following few pages, therefore, contain a few simple suggestions of how to begin to go after laughter.

A Sensitive Spirit

I believe that as long as we are not in a state of shock, there is always something to laugh about. What happens in what we label a serious situation, however, is that we turn off our humor antenna. The humor is there, but we don't see it. And even if we do find the humor, we often negate it and label it inappropriate. Yes, laughing at someone else's troubles is inappropriate. But sharing a laugh about some aspect of that trouble is not. So how do we determine what is appropriate and what is not?

Humor is appropriate if it comes from an *open heart*. I've always believed that is true, but I've recently heard another term that can also guide us toward appropriate humor. One minister, with a wonderful image, said, "if you use humor with a *sensitive spirit,* then it will turn out okay."

Using humor to poke fun at death is in bad taste if it puts down someone who is suffering. But appropriate humor—that which naturally comes out of adversity—gives those dealing with life-challenging situations power over a powerless situation. In fact, writer George Mikes points out that "laughing at death gives us triple pleasure: 1) the pleasure of the joke itself; 2) the malicious joy of laughing at death's expense; and 3) the pleasure of taming Death and fraternizing with him."

I agree with Mikes, but I believe appropriate humor in the death-and-dying process can provide even more—much more. You will see from the stories in this book how humor helped people cope; how it empowered them and how it was defiant, triumphant, and life-affirming; how it provided perspective and balance; and how it diverted their attention, gave them comic relief, and liberated them from their loss.

Humor can provide enormous benefits in tumultuous times. The problem is how to find it. Some suggestions follow.

• *Give people permission to laugh.*
"A lot of times, I'll ask a patient, 'Well, tell me, do you laugh?' Most of the time I get the answer, 'No way. I've got cancer, I don't laugh.' " So Lynn Erdman, R.N., director of Presbyterian Hospital's Cancer Center in Charlotte, North Carolina, then asks the patient, "Well, did you use to laugh?" Often the answer she gets this time is, "Oh, yes." Erdman then pops the $64,000 question: "Do you want it to stay the way it is now, or do you want it the way it used to be?" Ninety-five percent of the time, patients want more laughter in their life, so Erdman then shares this information with the family.

What Erdman does, in a very simple and effective manner, is give both the patient and the family, who may feel guilty or uneasy about laughing when their loved one is dying, permission to laugh together again.

One of Erdman's favorite humorous hospital-related stories concerned a woman who was dying "a slow but not painful death." The woman's daughters were vigilantly sitting by the patient's bed day and night. They were waiting for Mom to die. After several days, one of the sisters poked the other one and said, "How much longer do you think this is going to take?" At that point Mom opened her eyes, looked at the foot of the bed, where her two daughters were seated, and proclaimed, "A watched pot never boils."

The death-watch environment immediately changed as the woman and her two daughters had a good belly laugh. Mom died twenty minutes later.

• *Know the person.*

When my friend's sister had nose cancer, I sent her get-well wishes along with a red clown nose to cover her damaged one. My friend was upset. He thought I should not have done that. I, on the other hand, knew his sister and knew she would probably like it. I knew she had a leaning toward the outrageous because several times she really appreciated the funny and sometimes off-the-wall children's books I had given her in the past.

Nonetheless, because of my friend's comment, I thought that maybe I had indeed offended her. So I called to apologize. She was surprised at my call since she had been delighted to receive the gift and by the laughter it produced.

Several nurses I spoke with talked of the importance of establishing a sense of trust before humorous encounters can begin. They look for clues or openings from the patient. One nurse felt she needed to get to know the patient beyond just their dying body before any kind of true communication, including humor, could begin. For her, it was important to bring her own life challenges to each patient. Having had a battle with cancer herself, she knew well about patient anxiety. For instance, when she was ill, she felt that her life turned into "making out a will and changing it every four hours." Her daily concern, she said, became "who was going to get the steak knives after she was gone?"

The one thing that most caregivers stressed about the use of humor with the seriously ill was the importance of listening to a patient's feelings. Humor can help, they noted, as long as the patient knows that they are being heard. Humor used to negate the patient's wishes can be detrimental.

• *Look for the ludicrous.*

Harry Kondoleon, author of *Diary of a Lost Boy,* a funny novel about a dying young gay man and his straight friends, once said, "Dying, you see some things as quite beautiful and others as ludicrous." It's the ludicrous part, as Kondoleon points out, that makes moments in the dying process laughable.

For example, in a letter to *Ladies Home Journal,* cancer patient Carol Willis wrote about the bittersweet but inane advantages of dying: "I must be truthful and say there are a few advantages in living only half a lifetime. Besides the end of good, death also means the end of tribulations—no more holding in the stomach, no more P.T.A., no more putting up the hair in pincurls, no more cub scouts, no more growing old."

Another person told me that while they were visiting a terminally ill friend, who had only a month or so to live, the patient turned to them with a smile and said, "Well, I finally have enough money saved to last me the rest of my life."

And in *Reader's Digest,* one person wrote about an absurd incident that happened the day after a friend's mother had died: "The local library called to say that the book her mother had requested was now available. When my friend explained that her mother had died the previous day, the librarian said, 'Oh, would you like me to hold the book for three more days?' "

• *Can't laugh? Try smiling.*

When I was a hospice volunteer and was assigned to a new patient, I would sit in my car for five to ten minutes before I entered their home. There, I would do a smiling meditation. I would sit silently and center myself by focusing on smiling. I had read the hospice chart about the person I was going to visit but I never really knew what it would be like when I'd enter their home. So I did whatever I could to bring whatever lightness I could into the situation.

A smile is a way of connecting nonverbally with a person. As someone once remarked, "A smile is a light on your face to let someone know that you are at home."

Hurtful Humor

You have to be careful. The biggest thing I have learned through the years is that not everybody has a sense of humor.

—JONATHAN WINTERS

Humor is a funny thing. It can help but it can also hurt. Humor can break down barriers or build them, separate people or bond them, cut off communication or enhance it. We can laugh *with* someone or laugh *at* them—a minor difference in words but a major difference in outcome.

When we laugh at someone else's expense, we may enjoy the joke, but it only causes pain for the other person. Laughing at someone else creates animosity; we feel further apart. Laughing at a common enemy, on the other hand, like death or illness, bonds people together. We create a common experience; we feel closer.

There are many positive attributes to humor, but the negative list is just as long. Humor can gloss over things and conceal important information. It can mislead people so that they no longer believe you. Sometimes it backfires, and sometimes it can be painful to laugh.

HUMOR CAN BE A COVER-UP

Denial humor is a mixed bag too. As Kübler-Ross noted, denial can be helpful in the dying process. But it can also be hurtful. If, for example, the patient is continually joking about their illness to the extent that it precludes their getting treatment, then denial humor can be detrimental. Humor, after all, can be a healthy tool for temporary suppression but never for permanent repression.

Therapist Joanna Bull worked with Gilda Radner during the comedian's cancer days. In a magazine interview, Bull discussed Radner's use of denial humor, which had both a disadvantage and an advantage:

> Gilda . . . was the archetypal clown, able to find the funny side of any situation. As her therapist, this was sometimes difficult for me because she would often use it to avoid talking about deeper issues such as pain, loss of libido, altered image and fear of death. But I've learned through my years of working with cancer pa-

tients, that they all develop their own styles of coping with illness and I try to accept this. Gilda used humor to avoid looking directly at the frightening, sometimes overwhelming aspects of the illness.

One nurse I interviewed warned against the use of too much humor. She spoke of humor covering up a situation and not allowing a patient or caregiver to deal with the seriousness of what is happening.

She made an important point. Humor needs to be used for balance. McMurphy, the character in *One Flew over the Cuckoo's Nest,* says, "Man, when you lose your laugh you lose your footing." Very true. But overdoing humor, or using it as a cover-up, can be just as out of balance as not finding any at all.

HUMOR CAN BE MISLEADING

One of the problems with humor is that it can be misinterpreted. When we are laughing, people think that everything must be all right. But that is not always the case.

Genevieve Gipson, for example, one of the founders of the annual Nurses Assistant Day and Career Nursing Week, had a major car accident that left her life threatened. Sometime after the crisis had passed, she read her medical report. There she discovered that the emergency room doctor had written down, "Patient is not in acute pain—laughing and joking with the doctors." Gipson says, "The doctor perceived that if I could laugh and joke I was not in pain. Actually quite the opposite was true. One of the ways I coped with that period of time was to do the kind of joking that you don't have to think about too much. But the danger of laughter in such situations," Gipson reminds us, "is that others will put their own interpretation on it and they may differ from our own intentions."

HUMOR CAN BACKFIRE

Yes, humor can be beneficial. And, no, it doesn't always work. Sometimes it backfires. Here, for example, is a story from *Love, Laughter and a High Disregard for Statistics,* by Sue Buchanan. The author writes about visiting a business associate in the hospital who was recovering from plastic surgery.

I wracked my brain to think of some clever way to cheer her up and help her celebrate her new nose. . . .

First of all, I baked a cake—a scratch cake—and in retrospect I can see that I should have simply delivered the cake, expressed my good wishes, and left. It was the homemade get well card that caused the problem.

"Choose which nose you would prefer," I printed in bold letters on the front.

"A funny one?" it said on page two, where I pasted a picture of Mickey Mouse.

"A famous one?" it said beside Jacqueline Kennedy's photo.

"A political one?" beside Richard Nixon's mug.

There were other pictures and other blurbs, but you get the idea! The punch line, I'm sure you've already guessed: "Now that you've picked your nose, wash your hands and have some cake." I signed my name and set out to deliver the cake, chuckling all the way.

By the time I handed over my prize, I was smiling my toothiest smile. I couldn't wait for my friend to read the card. I waited for a reaction. I'm still waiting. She apparently saw no humor in it. No humor at all. I wasn't invited to stay for tea. I wasn't thanked. I didn't see her for days, and when I did, she was cool and didn't mention my card. To this day, every time I see her beautiful profile, I wonder how I could have missed so completely.

Sometimes It Hurts to Laugh

Studies have shown that reduction of anxiety prior to surgery helps postoperative recovery and the reduction of postoperative complications. Humor reduces anxiety and tension, so it can aid in this area, but as evidenced by the observation below, laughter after surgery can be painful.

"Humor is almost always great," Lisa, a woman from Texas, said, "but my personal experience following major surgery was that friends bringing humor into the hospital was not at all a funny thing—it resulted in my taking more morphine, not in my healing faster." The reason why humor was not appropriate was explained in Lisa's next sentence. "I had an eighteen-inch fresh incision in my abdomen. Laughter is not the best medicine in a surgical situation. No way around it. It just plain hurts, and it hurts a lot.

"Maybe laughter is a great healing in the hospital," Lisa concluded, "but not on the surgical unit—trust me on this one."

In the preceding chapters, we have seen how humor can be either helpful or harmful. In the following chapters, we focus on how those facing a loss find humor and how it helped them. Hopefully, through their encouraging and frequently funny stories, you too will find your laughing place and begin your own healing process.

Chapter 4

Lessons in Laughter

Death is always with us; creative art helps us know it, live
with it and even laugh at it.

—ROBERT LITMAN, M.D.

"I have good news and bad news," the doctor said. "The good news is you
have less than twenty-four hours to live."

"If that's the good news," exclaimed the patient, "what's the bad?"

The doctor replied, "I couldn't reach you yesterday."

One of the places we can learn that death is *not* too serious for humor
is from pop culture. Stand-up comedy, television sitcoms, movies, and cartoons know that death is appropriate laughing matter. In fact, one of the
functions of a comedian is to poke fun at those things that make us uncomfortable. A number of comedians, cartoonists, and writers do just that as
they joke about death. In doing so, they take the mystery out of it and present us with an alternative way of confronting our tears and our fears.

Comedians Laugh at Death

Is it not possible to argue, I ask, that our humorists and comedians are, without realizing it, modernized versions of Zen masters who teach us, entertain
us, and, at the same time, help heal us, or perhaps it is more accurate to say
help us heal ourselves.

—ARTHUR ASA BERGER, *An Anatomy of Humor*

In his book *SeinLanguage,* comedian Jerry Seinfeld describes death as "the last big move of your life." He writes, "The hearse is like a van, the pallbearers are your close friends . . . and the casket is that great, perfect box you've been looking for your whole life. The only problem is once you find it, you're in it."

Another comic, George Carlin, jokes that before we die, just as in a football game, we get a three-minute warning. Carlin advises us to use that warning well. He says, just after you get that signal, make the most outrageous and outlandish statement you have ever made. Then, just before the three minutes are up, look straight up and exclaim: "If that's not the absolute truth, may God strike me dead!"

A number of comedians, like Carlin and Seinfeld, touch on death-related topics in a humorous way. But no other comedian today has gotten us to look at, or laugh at, death as much as Woody Allen. Under the guise of tickling our funny bone, he has taken a not-so-funny subject and dealt with it in a way that is both funny and thought provoking.

Allen openly says things concerning death that we have kept buried deep within our consciousness. While Allen is bombarding us with laughter, he is questioning his own death and asking us to look at ours. He is constantly examining and denying his—and, in turn, our—fear of dying. He says such things as, "It's not that I'm afraid of dying, I just don't want to be there when it happens."

How come we can laugh at Allen's fears and foibles about death but have trouble joking about our own? For one, we get so caught up in the melodrama of our life-and-death struggles that we forget to see the inherent humor in them. Not so with Allen. Never is he so deep in his fears or neuroses that he cannot joke about them. He pokes fun at those things that bother him the most. "I don't believe in an afterlife," he quips, "although I am bringing a change of underwear."

We can laugh at Allen's humor about death because he juxtaposes life's larger, unanswerable questions (like death) with the nitty-gritty of everyday existence (like underwear) to create a comic absurdity. We thus laugh and, at the same time, realize the absurdity of his, and our, tenuous existence. By mixing the known with the unknown, we begin to get on familiar terms with our enemy; even death is not so threatening if we can bring it down to our level.

Death Knocks, a one-act play by Allen, is an excellent example of his fraternizing with death. In this short piece, Death enters the bedroom of Nat Ackerman by climbing in the window and nearly tripping on the windowsill. Death's opening line, typical of something any human being might utter in a similar situation, is, "Jesus Christ, I nearly broke my neck."

Suddenly Death is no longer the customary grim reaper but is, instead, a clumsy, out-of-breath entity who is not too unlike us or, for that matter, Nat himself. Because Death is brought to the human level, Nat is able to outwit him. After Death loses a game of gin rummy, he hastily exits, tripping down the stairs. Nat proclaims that Death is such a *schlep.*

In his analysis of Allen's work, autobiographer Maurice Yacowar tells us that because Ackerman does not recognize the power of Death, it has no power over him. Thus, we learn that by joking about our own death, we too can make it—or anything that oppresses us, for that matter—less frightening.

In the film *Annie Hall,* the main character, Alvy Singer, gives Diane Keaton a copy of Ernest Becker's *The Denial of Death* instead of the book about cats that she was contemplating buying. Singer tells her, "You should read this." Allen is constantly investigating and joking about his inevitable death because he knows, like Becker, that "the unexamined death is not worth living."

Allen's way of showing us how absurd our here-one-minute, gone-the-next existence is, is through humor. He even gets us to laugh at the ridiculousness that can arise out of trying to avoid death. In his film *Sleeper,* he pokes fun at both cryogenics, the freezing of the body to preserve life, and cloning, the duplication of body cells to replicate life.

After being awakened from a two-hundred-year deep freeze, Allen blurts out, "My doctor said I'd be in the hospital five days. My doctor was 195 years off." Later in the same film Allen mocks an attempt to duplicate the dead leader of the country by cloning him from the only part that still exists—his nose.

Allen continually expresses the death anxiety of all of us by questioning the meaning of life and why we are here. Yet underneath it all, Allen knows the answer. The key to life lies in enjoying it. In *Stardust Memories,* for example, Allen wants to write deeper, more meaningful material. The voices of a dozen or so Allen look-alike spacemen, however, command him, "Tell funnier jokes."

Although Allen knows that "life is divided into the horrible and the miserable," he also knows that the only way out of our suffering is through humor.

In *Hannah and Her Sisters,* the leading character believes that he will die soon of a brain tumor. Hopelessly depressed, he roams the streets of New York City. In his delirium, he wanders into a movie theater where a Marx

Brothers movie is playing. Like a reprieve from the hand of God, the images on the screen give him hope and strength. His message to us is that no matter how distraught we are, "we've got to enjoy ourselves while we are here."

Such is the message in his musical film *Everyone Says I Love You*. At the funeral home, the corpses get up from their coffins and join in a song-and-dance number. Their song? "Enjoy Yourself, It's Later Than You Think."

This message, of living fully in spite of knowing that one day we will die, is reiterated in Allen's movie *Love and Death*. One of the characters tells us, "You must not allow yourself to be consumed with grief. The dead are dead, life is for the living."

It is in the last image of this movie that Allen gives us his definitive answer regarding how to treat life and our ultimate demise. In the final moments of the film, Boris, the main character, is seen dancing side by side with a gossamer, white-clothed figure of Death. This image, says Yacowar, "is telling us that in the face of our mortality, we can do nothing better than snap our fingers, dance, laugh and be hearty."

Cartoonists Laugh at Death

With it [comedy] we can strike a blow at death itself. Or, at least, poke a hole in the pretentious notion that there is something dignified about it.

—JOHN CALLAHAN

Cartoonists use both visual and verbal exaggeration. They take everyday occurrences, add a twist, and suddenly the ordinary becomes extraordinarily funny. Like comedians, they too know that death is a suitable subject to scoff at. They poke fun at everything from the deathbed to the hereafter.

SOFTENING THE RAGE

In 1989, cartoonist Garry Trudeau created a three-week *Doonesbury* sequence about AIDS. While Trudeau's intention was to "attack the fear and ignorance by laughing in its face," many critics attacked him. In the cartoon, a former boyfriend of Joanie Caucus, one of the characters in the strip, is hospitalized with AIDS. At one point, a doctor tells the patient, "Your jammies clash with your lesions." Offensive? For a number of newspapers, it was; they refused to run the series. For Trudeau, however, it was another matter.

He was trying not only to educate the public in a medium they might actually listen to but also to show them that humor can "soften the rage."

In another strip, for example, the doctor says to Joanie, "Every day I go in to see Andy, and he makes some terrible joke about his lesions, and I play straight man, and we're both screaming inside, but it's better than going mad."

Andy, the cartoon character with AIDS, perhaps best expresses the message that Trudeau is attempting to get across to his readers. In the strip, he tells Joanie a joke:

"Have you heard what the original cause of AIDS was in San Francisco? Track lighting and gray industrial carpeting."

Joanie stares back in shock and asks, "How can you joke [at a time like this]?"

Andy, from his hospital bed, gives the definitive reply: "How can you not?"

How Does He Get Away with It?

An article in the *New York Times Magazine* stated that "cartoonist John Callahan makes fun of the blind, the crippled, people without arms or hearing." Then it asked, "How does he get away with it?" The answer is that he can get away with it because he is severely disabled. A high-speed car crash left him with limited use of his arms and paralyzed him from the diaphragm down. Callahan knows what it is like to be a quadriplegic, but he also knows that humorous cartooning is his salvation. "Humor," he says, "has become my way of coping."

The people that populate Callahan's cartoons come directly out of his pain. They are dismal—the disabled, the afflicted, the depressed, and the outcast—but his humor about them is bright. One cartoon, for example, shows a posse on horses hunting down an outlaw. When they come across an empty wheelchair, one of the men says to the other, "Don't worry, he won't get far on foot."

Another Callahan drawing comes straight out of a Hollywood western. Two cowboys are standing face-to-face ready for a gunfight. This time, however, there is a slight variation. One of the cowboys has no arms. As they are about to take their pistols from their holsters, the cowboy with arms warns the one without, "Don't be a fool, Billy!"

And in a third cartoon, one cowboy in a wheelchair is pointing his gun at another in a wheelchair while informing him, "This town ain't accessible enough for both of us!"

Callahan says, "I want to tell the handicapped to not take it so seriously and to never give up." Certainly Callahan hasn't. His outlook is as bright as the humor in his cartoons. When asked about his dating habits, for example, he says that since he is wheelchair bound, "I only flirt with girls who look like they have ground-floor apartments."

Hollywood Laughs at Death

I don't want to gain immortality through my films. I want to gain immortality through not dying.

—WOODY ALLEN

While Woody Allen may be the leading creator of films that contain the humorous side of death-related issues, he is not alone. From time to time, others in Hollywood have embraced this theme as well.

The Loved One, Evelyn Waugh's brought-to-the-screen novel, still stands as the ultimate spoof on the funeral industry. In it, a young English poet comes to Hollywood, where he gets a job at a pet cemetery. Soon afterward, he meets and falls in love with a woman who works as a cosmetician at another cemetery. She, however, is romantically torn between the poet and Mr. Joyboy, the chief mortician. In the end, however, neither wins her over, because her true love is none other than the funeral parlor itself.

This film, directed by Tony Richardson, was billed as "the motion picture with something to offend everyone." But even its critics thought that this macabre tale was very funny. Although they are fiction, in laughing at such films as *The Loved One* we get some comic relief from the ever-present threat of death.

Other movies have included various amusing views of funerals and the funeral industry. Examples include *Gates of Heaven* (featuring two California pet cemeteries), *Harold and Maude* (with its mischievous voyeurism at the funerals of strangers), and *S.O.B.* (where a mix-up in corpses provides the "little guy" with a big brassy send-off and the "big guy" with a simple cremation).

One of my favorite funny funeral scenes is from the movie *Steel Mag-*

nolias. In the film, a grieving mother is standing by the casket containing the corpse of her deceased daughter. She is naturally very upset over her loss and in her anger screams out, "I want to hit someone! I want to hit someone!"

Everyone has left the burial site except for the mother's small group of friends, standing a short distance away—one of whom is known for being very obnoxious. Someone pushes this woman toward the grieving mother and suggests, "Hit her. She hasn't done anything worthwhile in her life. Hit her!"

Perhaps one of Hollywood's most ambitious attempts to view all aspects and attitudes of dying in a humorous way can be seen in Robert Altman's film *The Wedding.* The movie takes place in a large home where an elaborate wedding is taking place downstairs while the grandmother is dying upstairs. At the very moment the bride and groom say, "I do," the grandmother takes her last breath.

Once the guests find out that a death has occurred, each one personifies some aspect of how people handle death. Many of their reactions, it turns out, are ludicrously funny. A priest, for example, enters the dead woman's room to routinely perform her last rites. Never is he aware, however, that she is already dead and can't hear one word of what he is preaching.

The amazing thing about this movie is that it hardly seems that we are watching a film about death. Altman convinces us that we are merely viewing a wedding party that has gone haywire. His humorous observations about people's relationship to a death, however, are brilliant.

Television Laughs at Death

Death is so *not* funny that it's funny.

—DANNY JACOBSON, cocreator of *Mad About You*

Laughing in the face of death is no stranger to television. For years, *M*A*S*H* has been poking fun at life-threatening medical emergencies. *The Mary Tyler Moore Show* won an Emmy for its death-related episode about Chuckles the Clown, and *Murphy Brown* struggled with finding a way to explain death to her young son.

Two other shows, *Sisters* and *Northern Exposure,* have had major humorous episodes that looked at both a life-threatening illness and death. We will explore both.

SISTERS

Daniel Lipman and his partner Ron Cowen were the producers of the first mainstream television movie to deal with AIDS. It was called *An Early Frost*. It softened this difficult and delicate theme by adding humor to it.

"It was such an incredible high"—Lipman says—when he won an Emmy for this program. "I called my mother, who I knew saw the show, and on this high that I was feeling, she tells me she has lymphoma. All at once I saw how the two trains of life, comedy and tragedy, were about to crash. And that," says Lipman, "is exactly what our voice on *Sisters* became." That show ran several seasons, with Lipman and Cowen as creators, producers, and writers.

One series of episodes on *Sisters* centered around the main character, Alex Halsey (impeccably played by actress Swoosie Kurtz), having a major medical problem. The opening script finds her perusing magazine ads and deciding that she wants bigger breasts. In examining her for breast enhancement, the doctor discovers a cancerous lump. Suddenly Alex is faced with having a lumpectomy or a mastectomy. She quips, "Ironic, isn't it? I mean, one day it's how much do you want them to give you, the next day it's how much do you want them to take?"

Alex jokes about her situation, but her sisters find nothing to laugh about. While they are having lunch, Alex orders a Suicide Sundae. "Well, don't look at me," she remarks; "I didn't name it. All I know," she continues, "is, in a couple of weeks, I'll be nuking and puking. So before I can't keep it down—I say, live it up!"

In her desire to do just that, Alex decides to throw a party for herself before she journeys into the world of chemotherapy and radiation. At the party, she has too much to drink. Inebriated, she entertains her guests by singing, "It's my party and I'll die if I want to, die if I want to, die if want to. You could die, too, if it happened to yoo-oo-oo!"

After chemo and losing her hair, Alex wants a wig that can magically transform her into someone else. In a fantasy scene, that magic happens. A breeze from the window blows open the yellow pages to Madam Sophie's Wig Shop. Madam's motto is "Transform yourself into someone else."

At the dusty old shop, Madam Sophie, a Dickensian character, informs Alex, "We give you a vig, and soon you vill be your old self again!"

"No, thank you!" Alex answers, "I want to transform myself—like your ad said. Be anyone but *me.*"

Madam Sophie gives Alex a box to take home, with careful instructions on how and when to wear the wig. At home Alex tries on the wig and becomes, at different times, a homeless bag lady, a passenger on the *Titanic,* and Marie Antoinette having her head chopped off. Finally, Alex winds up with hair that looks very much like her own.

The final script in the series finds Alex attending a support group. One day a friend of the group leader, Hildy Hirschberg, joins the group. Hildy, a stand-up comic played by comedian Elaine Boosler, is going to help the participants turn their cancer experience into a comedy routine.

At the second group meeting, Alex is coaxed by her new friend, Kate, into sharing something funny about her illness. Alex recalls a woman in the market who, knowing Alex was sick, gushingly remarked, "My dear, you are positively glowing."

"And I couldn't help it," says Alex; "the first thing that popped out of my mouth was, 'Of course I'm *glowing.* I just had radiation.'"

Several weeks later, while Alex is rehearsing the monologue she'll be performing at the comedy club, she learns that Kate has died. Upset, Alex angrily remarks, "Kate was dying, and we were making jokes! Whistling past the graveyard, la-dee-dah! Who did we think we were kidding? . . . I'm through laughing."

Kate's death is too much for Alex to handle. In spite of Hildy's beseeching her to go on with her monologue ("Who's gonna get the last laugh—you, or cancer?"), Alex refuses.

The night of the comedy show, Alex is nowhere to be seen until the very last minute, when she shows up quipping, "Sorry I'm late—but every time I get radiation, my watch stops."

Alex dedicates her performance to her friend Kate: "Actually, I've been lucky—if you can say 'lucky' and 'cancer' in the same sentence. I didn't lose my breast. Which is kind of a weird way of putting it—losing your breast. What does this mean? 'I was at Pricetown and my breast just wandered off by itself?'"

All of a sudden, you hear Alex imitating an announcer: "Attention, shoppers. We have a lost breast at Customer Service. Will the owner please report to aisle three."

The routine ends with Alex talking about one friend who bought her a lifetime membership in the Fruit-of-the-Month Club because the friend thought I'd "kick the bucket and she's off the hook."

"Well," says Alex with renewed hope, "I'm gonna be eating fruit salad for the next fifty years." And then, with a big, sly smile, Alex says triumphantly, "So, how do you like them apples?"

When I asked Lipman if he received any negative response to the cancer shows, he said, "None." The reason, I suspect, was that he handled them honestly and with humor. Because the shows used humor to deal with a serious situation, it was easy for the viewer to listen to, empathize with, and laugh along with the main character.

Through laughter, a number of important points were made about life-threatening illnesses. They are wonderful illustrations of what we will be discussing throughout this book.

First, like Alex, many patients find it easier to be lighthearted about their diagnosis than do their families and friends. The patient is using the powerful tool of humor to handle their adversity. Meanwhile, the family is wondering, "How can you possibly laugh at this?"

At one point in the script, several relatives are discussing whether Alex is using humor to deal with her illness or to deny it. Frequently patients do both. Yes, humor can help people cope with what they are going through, but it's also a way of them disowning it. Using denial humor may be the only way to get through a tough time without breaking down. If not taken to extremes, denial humor can prove to be a healthy coping mechanism when pain and suffering become overwhelming. Alex's drunken party scene is perhaps evidence that her denial humor may have gone too far.

The final, and perhaps most important, lesson in this series is that it's okay to get angry when someone you love dies, but it's not okay to let that loss end your life too.

Alex does not want to do her comedy routine after Kate dies. She feels she can't go on, with either the monologue or, for that matter, her own life. Somehow, however, she learns, as we all do, that she must go on—and humor helps her do just that. She dedicates her performance to her lost friend and triumphs over her tragedy.

> No subject is too serious for exemption from ridicule, not even death.
>
> —RON JENKINS, *Subversive Laughter*

NORTHERN EXPOSURE

Television, that great influencer of the masses, has played an important role in making death less somber. Like *Sisters,* the long-running TV show *Northern Exposure* also gives us clues on how laughter helps us live with loss. Christina J. Cicero analyzed a number of televised episodes in her thesis "The Treatment of Death and Dying in the Television Program 'Northern Exposure.' "

On one program, Ed, the young filmmaker, buys Ruth-Anne a mountain grave site for her seventy-sixth birthday. He says earnestly, "It's the gift that keeps on giving." Ruth-Anne, who seems pleased with her gift, asks Ed to dance with her on her grave. Then she comments dryly, "It's an opportunity of a lifetime."

The wry episode in which this appears, according to one newspaper article, "hints at a shift that's occurring in attitudes about death, from the traditional somber one to a more upbeat approach." The article attributes this change, in part, to the fact that we are forced to face death more often these days due to a greater number of young people dying of cancer and AIDS. It also points to the rise in baby boomers who are facing the death of their parents.

But why death issues on a comedy show? Because, as co–executive producer Andrew Schneider told Cicero, "the show deals with archetypal issues, death being one of them." These issues touch everybody, they are real, and they are, in some bittersweet way, frequently funny.

One script deals with fulfilling the burial wishes of a friend. The two surviving pals discover that the coffin they have built for their departed buddy is too small—apparently he had gained some weight since they last saw him. In another script, a one-hundred-year-old body is found frozen in a block of ice. The body is stored in the restaurant freezer, which has been cleared of mooseburger, while the townspeople decide what to do with their "refrigerated friend."

Another *Northern Exposure* episode revolved around Fleischman, the resident M.D., and the death of his uncle. Unable to attend the funeral, in Florida, Fleischman opts for saying Kaddish, the traditional Jewish prayer for the dead. To do this he needs to find nine other *Jewish* men. A simple task, perhaps, if he lived somewhere else, but near impossible in remote Cicely, Alaska.

To help Fleischman out, the townspeople search for Jews. First they discuss how they will know if someone is Jewish or not. Maurice notes, "The tip of the penis used to be an accurate indicator. But the widespread practice of circumcision has rendered that method of I.D. practically useless." Finally it is decided that they will use last names as a means of searching for Jews.

The townspeople begin. One of them tacks a flyer to a telephone pole: "Wanted—Members of the Jewish Faith." Another posts an all-points bulletin on the radio calling for "any and all children of Abraham."

One by one the townspeople import an unlikely crew of Jews—a lumberjack named Buck, an Englishman, and a converted Eskimo.

After a revealing dream, Fleischman finally calls off the search when he realizes the absurdity of praying with a group of strangers. He decides instead to say Kaddish with those he is closest to, his true family, the townspeople of Cicely.

Although the laughs come frequently, the examples cited above contain more than mere chuckles. According to Cicero, these shows educate us about our attitudes toward death and at the same time make us laugh. For example, says Cicero, in the episode about the death of Fleischman's uncle, we learn that "caring and support can emerge from unlikely and surprising sources," that "there is not *one* correct way of handling death," and that there is "the need for community . . . in the time of grief."

Only four *Northern Exposure* shows are mentioned here, but these, along with other death-related episodes, not only educate viewers about death attitudes but also show how laughter can make this unpleasant subject easier to confront.

Clowns Laugh at Death

It is that sometimes, through their antics, clowns can bring people back from severely withdrawn and unresponsive states even after all attempts by their doctors and nurses have failed.

—RAYMOND MOODY, *Laugh After Laugh*

Our final look at aspects of pop culture that present humor in the face of death involves the clown. We will examine both the clown as a healer and the clown's relationship to death. First, a story from the Jewish tradition that extols the clown's importance:

One day the prophet Elijah and a rabbi were standing in a courtyard. The rabbi inquired of Elijah, "Which ones in this courtyard are truly God's servants?" Elijah looked around and replied sadly that no one there could be considered God's servant. But then, in the far corner of the courtyard, they saw two men who were surrounded by a throng of people whose faces were smiling and laughing. Elijah approached these two men and asked them what they do. They told him they were clowns. They said that they make people laugh when they are suffering and they make peace between people when they are in conflict.

At that, Elijah turned to the rabbi and said, "These men are truly God's servants."

HEALING HARLEQUINS

While most of us are familiar with the circus clown, whose primary job is to entertain and make us laugh, there are other types of clowns as well. Clowns also visit hospitals to offer healing laughter to the seriously ill.

Clowns have a long tradition of easing the pain of both the ill and the bereaved. In ancient Rome, the court jester followed the funeral procession of his dead emperor in an effort to lighten up the public ceremony. In North America, clowns among the Pueblo, Hopi, Zuni, and Cree peoples were charged not only with entertaining fellow tribesmen but also with the important role of curing the sick by frightening away the demons of ill health. Today, clowns continue to work with the seriously ill and the dying.

In the August 1990 issue of *Life* magazine, there is a lengthy article about clowns in hospitals. Here is one segment about an encounter between a clown and a young patient:

> Dr. Pancake faced his greatest challenge when an 11-year-old Haitian boy named David Opont, doused with gasoline and set afire by a teenage delinquent, arrived in critical condition at New York Hospital's burn unit. "He was conscious but in terrible pain with major burns over more than half of his body," Dr. Pancake recalls. "I went right into emergency with him. When the surgeons began cutting away dead flesh, I began telling funny stories and promising circus tickets and making scarves appear and disappear, anything to keep his mind off the agony. Pretty soon he was rolling his eyes in amazement and finally I actually got him laughing behind his medical mask. It was incredible. He was staring death in the face—and he was having fun.

A similar story comes from Patch Adams, M.D. He is a "real doctor" and a "real clown" who runs the Gesundheit Institute in West Virginia. Every year since 1985, Adams has traveled to Russian hospitals, orphanages, and prisons to bring a bit of laughter to those who are hurting. He calls his mission Nasal Diplomacy in honor of his clown's bright red nose.

In the June 1994 edition of *Unity* magazine, Adams talked about the healing power of clowning:

Two years ago when we were clowning overseas, we stopped in Estonia and went to a children's burn hospital. I saw a woman in deep tears outside the door of a patient's room. I knew they were the tears of a mother whose child's life was in the balance. So I barged into the room. Estonia is a very poor country, and this hospital had practically no equipment. To my horror, there was a doctor and assistants working without any sterile techniques on a five-year-old boy with 65 percent to 70 percent third-degree burns from his chin down to his knees, completely encircling his body in that area. . . .

They were doing what they call debriding (cutting away dead tissue), which is extremely painful. . . . With no pain medication, this child was screaming bloody murder. With diligence and with great heroism, the doctor and two assistants were doing a magnificent job working against these odds. I was dumbfounded, not having a clue that the child couldn't move his head to see me. But soon after I entered the room, they had to move away, so I went over and looked down at the boy; he gave me a smile, and I later found out that what he told me just then was that I was beautiful. Believe me, my clown character is not beautiful but such are the ways of a child, and I spent the next hour and a half several inches from his face, clowning with him while they finished the procedure; he didn't scream out again. It was very emotional. I cry when I tell that story. It's one of the highlights of my life to have been there and to have been with the boy at that moment.

THE CLOWN/COMIC CONNECTION TO DEATH

The white-faced buffoon with a large red nose and baggy pants, the sad-eyed tramp with an overgrown beard, and the diamond-patterned Harlequin, as well as the stand-up/sitcom comic, have one thing in common. They have all tickled our funny bone at one time or another. What is not so well recognized, however, is that behind the slapstick and buffoonery lie connections to death.

Like the Fool in a deck of tarot cards, who is seen walking off the edge of a cliff with a serene smile on his face, the clown/comic can be battered with a slapstick or assaulted by verbal abuse, but he cannot be destroyed; he always comes back for more. He can flirt with death because he has nothing to lose.

When my wife knew that her death was imminent, she would not let anyone get away with anything. She thought nothing about confronting an obnoxious man who was honking his car horn outside our bedroom window at two o'clock in the morning. Because she had been told that she was terminal, part of her felt already dead. Thus, someone almost twice her height and weight could not frighten her. The clown/comic over whom death has no power vicariously gives us the experience of this kind of freedom.

Charlie Chaplin, the great film actor, realized the close connection between humor and death. Once he remarked, "I am always aware that Charlie is playing with death. He plays with it, mocks it, thumbs his nose at it, but it is always there. He is aware of death at every moment of his existence."

Even the language of today's stand-up comic is filled with death-related images. A comedian, for example, who is not doing well "dies" onstage; if the audience does not laugh, they are considered "dead." On the other hand, if the comedian is really funny, the audience "dies laughing" because he "knocked 'em dead"—and to top it off, it is the comedian's "deadpan" style that may have accomplished this.

Although a great deal of stand-up comedy may use *death* jargon, it is the circus clown that comes closest to our actual image of death. The parallel between the white face of the clown and the white face of the skeleton/ghost is obvious. Less obvious, but equally pertinent, is the fact that in certain third world cultures people paint their faces and decorate their bodies in a similar fashion, not for circuses but for funerals. The bushmen of Australia and several tribes in Africa, for example, do this to ward off evil spirits.

It is not too far-fetched to claim that the clown dresses in outlandish garb and paints himself with whiteface to ward off an evil spirit—the spirit of seriousness. Like the mourners from third world countries who decorate themselves, the clown sets himself apart from his audience by his appearance and calls attention to the fact that he has a special function to perform. By donning his "dead white" ghostliness, the circus clown both gets our attention and frightens us at the same time. We laugh at him from a distance but up close he becomes grotesque.

Death, too, is like that. We are at once fascinated and repelled by its image. We have learned to tolerate and even to poke fun at death when it is kept at bay, but should death come near, we hide our face.

Years ago, there was a dance performed by the Joffrey Ballet that revealed the true meaning of the clown/death connection. Appropriately, the ballet was called *The Clowns*. As the curtain rose, a heap of bodies, accumulated as if after some catastrophe, slowly start to come to life—one leg moves, a hand straightens out, a head rises up. Out of what appears to be total annihilation, new life starts to emerge. The mass of bodies slowly becomes a group of white-costumed, white-faced clowns. As the ballet continues, a promise of rebirth and renewal brings the seemingly dead clowns to life again.

The clown image in this ballet is truly what the clown image always is. Although the clowns' bodies are intertwined in death, their hearts nonetheless are connected to life. It is the clown, according to theologian Conrad Hyers, who "resembles a ghostly apparition from the spirit world, paradoxically seeking with grinning death-mask to renew life and revive our slumping spirits."

And so, with each laugh the clown/comic elicits from us, he reminds us that out of death can come an affirmation of life.

WHEN people experience a life-threatening crisis or a loss, they frequently get stuck—as in a Shakespearean drama—in the tragic fourth act. Tragedies end in ruin. Shakespearean comedy, on the other hand, puts things back together. "Comedies end in life and reunion," one writer explained. They "culminate in a feast, a marriage, a mood of celebration."

Life contains not only the tragic fourth act but the redemptive fifth act as well.

Welcome to act five.

Part II

Seeing

Demise Thru

Humorous

Eyes

Chapter 5

What's So Funny
About HAspitals?

I was real calm about the operation. 'Til I realized what I
was doing. I'm lying there naked. On a table in front of
people I don't know. And they have knives. What's wrong
with this picture?

— TOM PARKS

The Bizarreness of It All

While hospitals are far from funny places, they do tend to provide a breed-
ing ground for absurd occurrences. There is a certain inherent absurdness,
for example, in waking patients up to give them a sleeping pill, or in the standard, open-ended hospital gowns. (One cartoon I saw showing a large der-
riere sticking out of a hospital gown was captioned, "Now I know why they
call it I.C.U.") The following anecdotes exemplify some of the bizarre
humor that occurs amid the life-and-death stuggles encountered in hospital settings.

One woman, for example, told me:

My late husband was in the intensive care unit, heavily med-
icated and on a respirator. He had tried to write a note to his
mother, who couldn't make out his handwriting. After passing
the note around to the other relatives, they all decided that his
note said, "I don't like the respirator. Take me off."

Since I had the power of attorney, they called me to come down to the hospital immediately. When I saw the note, I knew their interpretation was off, but I couldn't tell, either, what was meant. After a few moments trying to get him to tell me what he wanted, a nurse walked in and Ric pointed to the nurse and then back at the pad. Suddenly, it all became clear!!

He had written, "I don't like that nurse. Get him out."

I thought I wouldn't be able to stop laughing! Here his family was ready to pull the plug, and he was just commenting about a nurse who was always late with his morphine!

DEAD OR ALIVE?

Inspirations for Caregivers by Leslie Garfield provides another example of a bizarre hospital incident:

When I was a student nurse, a story was told about one of my classmates who went to get her patient ready for physical therapy. He had just had a stroke and was not much help with the transfer. She had finally gotten him into a sitting position and was about to call for assistance when the doctor came in the room. The M.D. asked what she was doing. She said that she was getting the patient up for physical therapy. "That's strange," said the doctor. "I was coming in to sign the death certificate."

THANK YOU NOTES

The following story, told to me by my friend Dana Gribbin, takes place in the South, where hospitality and graciousness are bywords. And where, says Gribbin, "My mother, bless her heart, did her best to rear us as proper Southern ladies."

Several years ago, Gribbin's mom had just come through a major operation, one that unfortunately did not fully accomplish what it was intended to do. Her mother did not have long to live.

"In my bedside conversation with her," Gribbin laughingly recalls, "I, for some reason, mentioned the word *belly*. Being the very proper Southern woman she was, Mom didn't like me using that word. But I said, 'Mom, what do you want me to call it, *stomach dancing?*'" Gribbin says, "I laughed a lot when I thought about the absurd contrast of the very severe circumstance and my mother worrying about me using the word *belly.*"

At one point in her mom's illness, Gribbin had to leave her mother in an East Coast hospital and return to the West Coast. She hired sitters to be in the room with her mom. Knowing that this might be the last time she would see her mother, and possibly the last time she would hear her mom speak, Gribbin leaned over to say good-bye. In doing so she thought perhaps she would hear some final words of wisdom. Her very proper Southern mom, however, who hadn't been able to speak up until this point, drew her daughter close to her and then reminded Gribbin, "Be sure to write thank-you notes to the sitters."

....

A ninety-two-year-old woman suffered a full cardiac arrest at home and her family called for an ambulance. The ambulance transported the patient with CPR in progress.

She arrived in our ER and, after thirty minutes, we were unable to resuscitate her. I pronounced her dead and went out to tell her seventy-eight-year-old daughter.

I looked at her gently and said, "I'm sorry, ma'am, but your mother didn't make it."

Shocked, she looked at me and shouted, "Didn't make it? Where could they be? She left in the ambulance forty-five minutes ago!"

—GEORGE R. DREW, D.O.,
in Mark Brown, *Emergency!:
True Stories from the Nation's ERs*

....

A Certain Shocking Audacity

"Most of us do not associate hilarity with the hospital," writes Marilyn Chandler, discussing examples of books that touch upon humor in illness. "It seems a little hard-hearted to be in any way light-hearted about crippling diseases," she says. "We tend to approach serious illness in a serious vein, and appropriately so. Most of us would agree that no one has a right to laugh unless it is the victim. And even then," Chandler continues, "it takes a certain shocking audacity to leave your tongue in your cheek when you speak words like cancer and death."

Many of the people quoted in this chapter are patients who had "a certain shocking audacity" to laugh in the face of death or serious illness. And thank God they did. For in their boldness, they show us how humor helped them cope with their illness and possible imminent death.

Hospitals, as Chandler points out, are not the most joyous of places. Still, humor does play an important role in spite of, or perhaps because of, the life-and-death struggles that happen there. In a study of a hospital ward where the majority of the patients had incurable diseases, researcher Renee Fox found that patients frequently joked with one another about their isolation, their incapacity, their surgeries, or the medical apparatus.

One patient defiantly joked, "I think the reason I'm so fouled up is because of all the gooey stuff they're always sticking in my veins. . . . What I need is an I.V. of Sani-Flush." In another instance where intravenous (I.V.) was used frequently, patients jokingly called themselves the "hall of I.V."

Many of the patients that Fox studied were near death's door. She reports that their humor was a way of "looking [death] straight in the eye" and trying to overcome it. The stories in this chapter are a testament to the inventiveness of patients, like the ones Fox interviewed, who had the audacity to find humor in a hospital setting.

But My Nose Blew Itself!

In an extremely funny book titled *How Am I Gonna Find a Man If I'm Dead?*, author and cancer patient Fanny Gaynes writes about the not-so-funny world of cancer and the absurdity she encountered during her many hospital stays. After her bone-marrow transplant, she notes:

> And then there were rules for *avoiding* infection. These had to be followed *at all costs*. I could do nothing that might break my skin, even unnoticeably. Now that I had no white blood cells to fight infection and very few platelets to help me clot, simple acts that I'd always taken for granted—brushing my teeth, opening my mail, filing my nails, blowing my nose—could kill me.
>
> So I brushed my teeth with little "Toothettes"—soft, pink, spongy things that look like what you'd use to wash dollhouse dishes. Somebody else opened my mail. My nails, well, they just grew off the map. And my nose, my nose—God, my nose drove me crazy. Not being able to blow it was like having an itch that *no one* could scratch.

Early one morning, before David arrived, my nose just sort of started running. Which reminded me of my favorite Martin Mull line, "Noses run in my family," which made me kind of laugh/snort, which made my nose run some more, which made me want to blow it so badly I could (you should pardon the expression) taste it. I decided to take a piece of Kleenex and just pat it: after all, that wouldn't exactly be "blowing," per se. But once that Kleenex got in the vicinity, oh, God, please forgive me, I gave the eensy weensy teensiest honk and, before I knew it, my nose was blown.

When David arrived I blurted with a mixture of glee and relief: "I blew my nose!" But then he glared at me like a father catching his three-year-old using a chain saw to slice a bagel, and I knew I was in trouble.

I was so ashamed of breaking the rule that out of my mouth fell—with the innocence and intensity of a child who once told me that her "pencil made a mistake and broke"—what I, under pressure, believed to be TRUTH, "I don't know what happened, David: my nose, it just blew itself."

Hearing me blame my nose for attempted murder, we both broke into prolonged fits of laughter—causing my nose to blow itself again.

And *this* moment, I'm sorry to report, was the highlight of my transplant.

....

Joni would be returning to Omaha that evening. Knowing how passionate she was about decorating, I immediately angled my hospital bed and Barcalounger chairs.

And lucky I did. At 6:00 sharp my fanatic fairy-godmother friend twirled through the door with a fleet of peach and seafoam-green decorating items—pillows, comforters, throws, rugs, lamps, paintings, picture frames, jars—and whipped that place into such amazing shape that within minutes I was praying my room would go condo.

—FANNY GAYNES, *How Am I Gonna Find a Man If I'm Dead?*
....

In one chapter of her book, Gaynes asks, "What is that thing within us all that sustains us through nightmares we never dreamed we could bear?" For Gaynes, it was obviously courage, tenacity, and without a doubt, humor.

CRITICAL CARE

Dr. Steve Allen Jr., son of the comedian Steve Allen, tells a delightful story about the time his dad was in the hospital. Allen Sr. had just had surgery for colon cancer. Two days into his postoperative recovery, he received what was for him an excess dose of morphine. His breathing and respiration fell to substantially low levels, and because of the morphine, he relaxed—a lot.

Allen Sr. recalls hearing a Code Blue over the PA system. He couldn't hear the room number but he thought to himself, "Some poor schnook is unfortunately at death's door."

Suddenly a team of paramedics filled his room. Allen finally realized that the Code Blue was for him and this might be his last thought. In the midst of all of this chaos, a quiet woman who was standing in the doorway called out, "What's his condition?—so that I can notify the family." The physician yelled back, "His condition is critical, of course."

In spite of his serious medical status at the time, Allen recalls thinking, "Sure, I'm critical. I'm critical of the food. I'm critical of the nurses. I'm critical of the doctors—and it's going to cost too much too!"

People who can laugh can cope better with serious illness.
—JOHNATHAN GOLDMAN, M.D.

THE RAUCOUS RECOVERY ROOM

Annette Goodheart is a psychotherapist and seminar leader who presents most of her programs on laughter with a twenty-seven-inch stuffed animal named Charlie Bear. "Charlie's an expensive bear," Goodheart says, "but a very cheap relationship."

Goodheart believes that both tears and laughter are cathartic. They cleanse the body and the soul and help us get rid of pent-up, harmful tension. In *Laughter Therapy*, Goodheart writes about how they helped her when she underwent surgery:

> In the early seventies, I needed to have a D&C. The procedure was such that it could be done on an outpatient basis. I arranged with my gynecologist to have a local anesthetic so I could be alert and aware during the process. He agreed and set the date.
>
> At dawn, as my friend was driving me to the hospital, I

began to cry. I cried (for whatever reason) for the twenty-minute ride. After I got to the hospital, undressed, and climbed into bed, the nurse came in and took my blood pressure. She looked at me with great alarm and took my blood pressure again. She quickly left the room and returned with the physician, who then took my blood pressure, looked at me quizzically, and told me that if I were any more relaxed I would be dead. I had had no drugs at this point, but the crying had so relaxed me and rebalanced the chemistry from my stress that my blood pressure was unusual for someone anticipating surgery. . . .

After the surgery was over, I was rolled into the recovery room. . . . Feelings of isolation and loneliness swept over me as I lay on my back, unable to move my legs, waiting for the anesthetic to wear off. . . .

At this point, a friend who is notorious for her nerve opened the recovery room door. The nurses scurried over and told her that no visitors were allowed. She said, "But I am her personal counselor!" (She lied.) They were caught so off guard that they said, "Oh, okay," and in she came to my curtained alcove.

As soon as I saw her, we started to laugh. Immediately the nurses caught on and made her leave, but it was too late. I couldn't stop laughing. I laughed and laughed and laughed, all by myself, lying flat on my back, surrounded by what the nurses had hoped to be a separating wall. I was laughing so hard that they immediately wheeled me out of the room and upstairs to my bed, without waiting for the physician's okay. So I truly laughed my way out of the recovery room.

When You Gotta Go, You Gotta Go

> You no longer die in the hospital, you merely experience "negative patient outcome."
>
> —Bob Ross

Art Gliner, like Goodheart, is a pioneer in teaching people about the benefits of humor and laughter. Recently he had to find some for himself, when he was dealing with the last nine months of his mother's life. Much of the laughter, he found, came from absurdity.

"During the night," his mother said, "I got up to go to the bathroom." Just as she was about to return to her bed, her roommate ran into the bathroom and in an agitated voice insisted she pull the cord to summon the nurse.

"Why should I do that?" she asked.

"Because," the roommate told her, "there is a man in your bed!"

Sure enough, a man from a room across the hall had become confused and wandered into the room and plopped himself on the bed.

"And," said Gliner's mother, "he was stark naked! Two minutes later and he would have plopped down on top of me."

Much of the humor that Gliner experienced with his mother during these difficult times came from the interaction they had with each other. Frequently he would tell her that she might feel better if she would try this thing or that thing. Invariably she would scold him and reply, "You are practicing without a license."

"One day," says Gliner, "my mother was giving me the latest rundown on her ills. She said, 'These pains are coming more often today.'" Then, remembering that Gliner told her that it might be a good idea if she didn't complain so much, she caught herself and remarked, "It must be because I'm pregnant."

Gliner says that he is fortunate to have many fond (and funny) memories of his mother, memories that will always be with him, especially her idea of mortality—"Dying," she said, "is like going to the bathroom. When you gotta go, you gotta go."

Ten Minutes of Belly Laughter

There is always a margin within which life can be lived with meaning and even with a certain measure of joy, despite illness.

—Norman Cousins, *Anatomy of an Illness*

Several years ago, I was one of the panelists on a couple of closed-circuit teleconferences. Norman Cousins was also on the panel. Cousins was the editor of *Saturday Review* for many years and the author of several books, including *Anatomy of an Illness*. In that book, he discusses the laugh therapy he used to cure himself of a life-threatening illness, and his discovery that ten minutes of genuine laughter gave him two hours of pain-free sleep.

I recall Cousins making an unusual statement during one of the teleconferences. He said that it was the patient's responsibility to lighten up a hospital experience. Perhaps Cousins felt this way because he knew, as we all do, that when we are hurting, if we can make others laugh and feel better, then we often feel better too.

Cousins's classic example occurred during one of his hospital stays. He says, "The nurse came in with a specimen bottle at a time when I was having breakfast. While she wasn't looking, I took my apple juice, poured it in the bottle, and handed it to her. She looked at it and said, 'We're a little cloudy today, aren't we?' " Taking the bottle back from the nurse, Cousins held it up to the light, took a swig from the bottle, and declared, "By George, you're right; let's run it through again."

CHAOS INTO COMEDY

A number of people I've interviewed or have read agree with Cousins that patients need to take an active role in brightening up their hospital stay. No patient did it better, though, than the self-proclaimed "court jester of the counter culture and holy house clown of the cosmos," Wavy Gravy.

In *Something Good for a Change,* Wavy Gravy (aka Hugh Romney) says, "All through my life I have attempted to turn adversity into an ally. And chaos into a comedy." He even managed to do this when confined to a hospital bed. Here are some of his suggestions for adding more mirth to medical institutions:

> First thing I do whenever I check into a hospital is to decorate. I start off with tie-dyed sheets and a little puja table (or altar), where I always arrange my reminders of Heaven. A candle, some incense, and statues of Buddha, Jesus Christ, and Donald Duck. All my chrome bedguards are entwined with fake vines and artificial flowers. I try to make the hospital a fun place to be in.
>
> One night a new nurse came into my room about dawn and just went crazy. She let out a long piercing scream and went careening down the hallway in quest of the intern on duty. It seems this was her first encounter with tie-dyed sheets and she thought I had bled funny.

I have discovered others like Wavy Gravy and Norman Cousins who consciously used humor to ease their hospital experience. Several used notes, stickers, and messages written directly on their body to create some comedy before their surgery.

In an article entitled "Jest for Your Health," published in the magazine *Healing,* nurse Patty Wooten describes what one patient did:

> Mr. Barnes was scheduled for abdominal surgery. He was anxious—scared of the unknown, the pain and specially the strangers, who would invade his body. Perhaps if he could feel a connection with those strangers in masks, he could relax. A friend visiting him the night before surgery provided the solution. The next morning, Mr. Barnes arrived in the operating room grinning from ear to ear. Soon after the staff began preparing him for surgery, they started to laugh. On his belly they found a sticker requesting, "Hey, Doc, while you're in there could you check the oil?" The staff congratulated Mr. Barnes on his joke and eagerly awaited the arrival of the surgeon, who quickly joined in the laughter. Everyone felt a sense of relaxation and camaraderie as they laughed together and shared the joy. As Mr. Barnes drifted into sleep, he knew he was among friends.

But that's not the end of the Barnes story. Wooten writes, "After the surgeon completed Barnes's surgery, he placed a strip of tape on the bed with these words, 'Oil checked, tires rotated. Next inspection tomorrow morning or 30,000 miles, whichever comes first.' "

Happy Birthday, Doc

In her book *Love, Judy: Letters of Hope and Healing for Women with Breast Cancer,* author and cancer patient Judy Hart also talks about what she did prior to her surgery:

> The bone marrow doctor noticed I had a birthday coming up and commented that so did he. In fact, the date is the day for which my bone marrow harvest had been scheduled.
>
> I go to Pre-Op Testing. . . . After covering my list of questions and requests, including one for my anesthesiologist, I say to the nurse, "I have a question you may not have heard before."
>
> "Unlikely, Judy," she says, shaking her head, "but let's hear it."

"I want to know if there's a way, consistent with the need for a sterile field, to write 'Happy Birthday!' to my doctor on my backside."

"Número uno," she answers. "Nobody has asked that one before. And it's easily done. I'll give you a special pen surgeons use to mark the body. Have your husband do it before you leave the house tomorrow morning."

Before our 5:30 A.M. departure, John letters my backside in pizzazzy purple. Despite my playfulness, I feel anxious . . . it is not until I'm in the final holding room, sharing my backside with the anesthesiologist, that I lose my malaise. Now as I laugh and relate, I feel myself calming. . . . I charge the anesthesiologist with making sure the message is seen by the birthday doctor.

Some hours after the surgery, it is the non-birthday doctor who comes first to see me. I ask if they got my message. "Indeed we did and we wrote one back. You'll have to get a mirror."

For a mirror, I use my nurse. She read "Happy Harvest and No Returns."

Thank you, purple-penned prose. Thank you for giving me a project during an uncomfortable time and for ripples of laughter from a whole line of medical helpers.

You Could Hear a Stethoscope Drop

In her book *Still Talking,* comedian Joan Rivers writes about the humor she consciously created to ease her stress when her husband Edgar was in the hospital. Here is what she did:

> One night at 2:00 A.M. I was there beside Edgar, and Bill Sammeth came by. We began helping the nurse make cold packs by filling rubber gloves with ice. Then we got silly and blew up the gloves into balloons. With people dying around us, the long, shadowy room lit only by a light at the nurse's desk and the green glow of computer screens—Billy and I laughed hysterically as we hit five-fingered balloons back and forth across my husband's body. Totally macabre.
>
> When a situation becomes *really* awful, I get silly and laugh, make it absurd. The laughter helps me convince myself, "I can get

through this." I feel a lightness, a release. I suppose that is why I am a comedian—I can do that for myself and for audiences.

Another time Billy and I were riding down in an elevator crowded with doctors. Suddenly Billy turned to me and said, "They sued him and they won. The man doesn't have a house, a car, doesn't have any practice left." The elevator became very, very quiet. "I would be a witness all over again after what that butcher did," Billy went on, "and I actually enjoyed lying on the stand." You could hear a stethoscope drop. I tried to remember everything funny that happened so I could make Edgar laugh when he woke up.

Jon Carroll, a columnist for the *San Francisco Chronicle,* wrote that "the humor we find in tragedy is sometimes all that makes life tolerable." The people quoted in this chapter know that being in a hospital is far from funny. But they also know that funny things happen there. In one way or another, they were able to find something to laugh about to make their hospital experience a bit more tolerable.

Chapter 6

Hospice:
Serious? Yes.
Solemn? No Way!

Lightly, my darling, lightly, even when it comes to dying.
—ALDOUS HUXLEY

Humor and the
Hospice Patient

The word *hospice* comes from a Latin word meaning a place of shelter. Today, hospices around the country provide a haven for dying patients. Because the patient has little time left, the focus of hospice is not cure but care—to make the patient as comfortable and as pain free as possible.

Most people are familiar with the hospice concept these days. When I was a hospice volunteer, however, this was not the case. I recall one nurse going out to give a lecture about hospice care and coming back in hysterics. Several people in the audience were aghast that she would be discussing death. They thought the talk was to be about cooking with "hot spice."

I became one of the first of twelve volunteers with the newly formed Hospice of San Francisco a year-and-a-half after my wife died. It was the first hospice in the city and one of the first in the country; now there are nearly two thousand hospices nationwide.

During my volunteering days, many of my friends thought working with the dying was a morbid task. I had a hard time convincing them otherwise. Yes, there were sad times, but they never outnumbered the rewards. And the rewards were many. Each and every patient gave me a gift. I always felt enriched by my encounters with them. Those near death taught me about life.

From one patient, for example, I learned about giving. Classical music was her passion. She had bought season tickets to the symphony, but as the opening of the concert season grew closer it was clear that she was much too ill to go. The hospice team talked about taking her to the symphony on a gurney, but even that didn't seem feasible, considering her condition.

Then, in one hospice support team meeting, we came up with a possible solution. If she couldn't get to the symphony, maybe the symphony, or part of it at least, could come to her.

I called the San Francisco Conservatory of Music and told them the story. They offered to have one of their graduate students come to her home. The following night, the patient and her family were treated to a private violin concert. Later, her son told me that it was a truly magical experience—and one of the last joyful times the family spent together.

From another patient, I learned about forgiving—and about lightening up. Every time I'd visit, this elderly woman would be lying on the couch half asleep with the television blaring away. I tried chatting with her, but because of the noise from the TV, that was impossible.

I was a new hospice volunteer and I desperately wanted to do something for this patient. So, one day, when I thought she was sleeping, I got up and lowered the TV.

"What are you doing?" she demanded.

"I'm just lowering the volume so we could talk," I said.

"Make it louder," she shouted.

So I did, and then, to be heard over the TV, I yelled, "I'm here to help. Is there anything I can do for you?"

There was a long silence and then she asked, "Do you know how to dance?"

"Yes," I said.

"Well, get up and dance," she replied.

Being a new volunteer, I would have done practically anything for the patient. So I got up and danced around the room to the music of *The Dating Game*.

Feeling a bit better about being able to fulfill the patient's wish, I asked her how she liked my performance.

First, there was no reply. Then she simply shrugged her shoulders.

Still feeling frustrated about wanting to help her, I again asked, "Is there anything else I can do for you?"

After another long pause, she replied, "Do you know how to disco?"

So I got up and disco danced around the room again and asked her how she liked it this time. She shrugged her shoulders once more.

"Listen," I persisted. "I'm a volunteer. I'm here to help. Isn't there anything I can do for you?"

There was another long silence and then she said, "Yes there is. You can leave!"

My heart sank as I held back my tears. When her family returned I went back to the hospice office and told them the story. They convulsed with laughter.

"What is so funny?" I said.

"If only you could see yourself dancing around the room to *Dating Game* music, you would laugh too." And in hindsight, I did.

I also realized, as I forgave her, that I was the only one toward whom she could express her anger. There were only six people in her entire life at the time—her son, daughter, doctor, nurse, home health care aide, and me. I was the low man on the totem pole. She could do without me but not without the others.

This woman taught me a great lesson about working with the dying. The most important thing I could do for a patient, when so many others might turn away, was to just be there. If the patient wanted to sleep on the couch while the TV was blaring, great. If they wanted to talk about death, great. If they *didn't* want to talk about death, great. If tears came up, great. If laughter came up, great. There was really nothing special I needed to do. After all, it's not my agenda, it's theirs.

As is so frequently the case, the patient is obliged to play comforter, to alleviate the alarm and panic of concerned companions, and to take responsibility for creating an atmosphere of hope in the midst of panic.

—MARILYN CHANDLER, "Healthy Irreverence"

PLAYING COMFORTER

While investigating hospice humor, I noticed that it came primarily from two sources—the staff and the patient. Rarely did the family find anything to laugh about.

The humor initiated by the patient struck me as being most unusual—not because someone who was dying was able to joke about it, but because it was often a way of them taking care of the caregiver. In the guise of kidding around, patients were saying, "It's okay. I know I'm dying. I know it is stressful for you, but don't worry, it's going to be all right."

Anyone who teaches knows that they frequently learn the most from their students. It is no different in the patient/caregiver relationship. In spite of what the patient is going through, they are the one who teaches those around them how to lighten up.

Patty Wooten, R.N., remembers the time she learned this lesson while caring for a patient in the intensive care unit. "A ninety-two-year-old man was bleeding profusely and I'm running wild," she says. "I have him on all these medications, I'm taking his blood pressure, I'm monitoring his urine output, I'm cleaning the bed—I'm just running wild. Then, at about 3 A.M., five hours after my shift started, he reaches over the bed railing for my arm and says, 'Relax, sweetheart, everybody's got to die sometime.' "

Wooten says that there was an ironic, whimsical kind of thing happening—"I mean, who is taking care of who here?"

In Wooten's first book, *Heart, Humor and Healing,* Donna Strickland, R.N., provides an excellent example of how one patient took care of her:

A nurse on the hospice unit asked me to visit a dying man who needed to talk "about death." I was exhausted but agreed to try. I walked into this room and became acutely aware that death lurked. I noticed that the man was about 6 ft. tall and weighed 80 pounds. I had never seen anyone so thin. I was scared. I put my hand out and said "Hi. The nurse asked me to talk with you about death." I smiled stupidly. (What had I just said? I never talked like that.)

He looked up at me with the bluest, brightest eyes I had ever seen. He said, "Looks like you've had a pretty rough day!"

"Yes," I replied. There was silence. My eyes swelled with tears. I apologized for the way I entered the room and he interrupted me with, "It was last week I was concerned about death. I'm not anymore. Hey, why not sit down and let me tell you my favorite joke?"

Tears streamed down my face. Tears began filling my eyes. "What has 75 balls and drives old ladies crazy?"

"Oh, good Lord, what?!"

"Bingo!"

We laughed as if it were the best and finest joke either of

us had ever heard—and we cried as if there were no tomorrow. I left his room knowing that I had been given a rare gift of a lifetime.

WE WANT TO LAUGH

"I try to be playful but others won't respond."
"If I ever needed humor it is now."
"I want to smile and laugh, but that upsets my family."

The comments above are from hospice patients. They were gathered by Kaye Ann Herth, Ph.D., R.N., who interviewed fourteen terminally ill adults with a prognosis of six months or less to live. Eighty-five percent of the patients in this study thought that humor would be helpful at this time, but only 14 percent indicated its presence.

Herth found that humor had a number of positive attributes for hospice patients. Here, summarized, are some of her findings:

• *Humor helped a patient's self-esteem*—participants felt like "a real person again" because they were sharing something positive.
• *Humor altered a patient's attitude*—it enabled them to see things more positively and helped them "put a new light on their situation."
• *Humor aided a patient's communication*—it "allowed them to ask questions that they might otherwise not ask and to hear instructions they might otherwise be too anxious to hear."

Although this was a relatively small study, its importance is immense. Those attending the dying need to be more aware of the positive value of humor and how life-affirming it can be even in the face of death. "Over and over again," Herth says, "the participants expressed that humor enabled them to feel 'alive' and thus for them was a life-enhancer and life-enricher even though their time was very limited."

In spite of the fact that hospice patients might want more humor, it may not be easy to achieve. I thus asked one hospice nurse for some clues on how to do this. She said, "I try to change the subject [of illness and death] a lot. I try to introduce a different aspect of life. It is so easy for the patient to be sidetracked into their problems, their dying. When emphasis is taken off the dying process, they become more of their old person again. They are then more open to joking around."

I reminded my mother that I asked her to stop calling because she'd only call when she was depressed. "I know you may get depressed when you think of me, but don't call. Wait until you are upbeat and in a good mood. Dying is painful enough for me without taking on your pain too," I said.

—ROBERT DEANDREIS, writer with AIDS, in *Sentinel* newspaper

WAIT FOR THE FUNERAL

In *Someone You Love Is Dying,* Martin Shephard, M.D., writes about his father's illness. He recalls a conversation with his dad in which his father reveals his wanting to be treated as a person rather than as someone who is already dead. Shephard's father handles this frustration, as many patients do, with some humor.

> Oh, yes. I found to my dislike, that people show up very sympathetic, very nice, and sort of pity me. I could never take that. My friends, my very good friends and relatives, were sincerely frightened. They just don't like to see a situation of this sort, and they really felt bad. . . .
>
> I will give you an example. My cousin and I are very close. When she came to the hospital to see me, she took it so bad that she left the room and started to cry. I knew that, so I put my gown on and followed her. It seems she just could not take it. She felt as if it was a funeral. I said, "Look. I got a few more months. Wait for the funeral." I even joked about it. I had a good laugh. . . .
>
> Yes, I never lost my sense of humor. . . . I still enjoy life. I know I am going to die. I don't know when. But somehow, back in my mind, I also think I am going to lick this. Maybe I can urinate on my doctor's grave.

AN OPEN DOOR POLICY

Carol McDowell is a certified grief counselor who "believes in life." McDowell runs a loss-and-laughter group for widows and widowers. One of its male members liked to share jokes with her. This was his favorite:

Three guys, who bonded in college, continued to be close friends the rest of their life. They moved to the same town, worked in the same factory, and lived though the death of each wife.

Now retired, the three men spent every Saturday morning sitting on the park bench and talking about life—and death. Curious about what the hereafter might be like, they make a pact. The first one to die will come back and tell the other two what it is like.

Joe dies shortly after. The two return to the park bench every Saturday waiting for Joe to fulfill his part of the agreement. Finally, they hear a voice in the bushes: "Pete? Mike? Is that you?"

"What the heck took you so long?"

"Well, I tried to get here but there is nothing but sex, sex, sex . . ."

"What, are you in heaven?"

"Heaven? No way. I'm a rabbit in Ohio."

In the course of time, McDowell's joke-telling friend became very ill. He wasn't expected to live much longer. Since she had to leave town and knew that he might not make it until she returned, McDowell went to say good-bye.

"Look," she said, "if you are here when I get back, great. But if not, I understand."

"No," the man answered, "I don't think I'll be here. I'm going to die."

"Then do me a favor," McDowell asked. "Remember the joke about the three men on the park bench? Well, why don't you come back and tell me what's it's all about?"

The patient looked at McDowell and said, "I'll do something even better. I'll leave the door open for you!"

For the hospice patient, humor can be a way of dealing with such things as failing body functions, unfamiliar medical procedures, and confused emotions. Humor can give the terminally ill a sense of power when all else seems hopeless. The patient may not have much control over the nearness of death, but they do have the power to joke about it.

Humor and the Hospice Staff

"On the face of it," says Dennis Sibley, a former hospice nurse in England, "a hospice seems an unlikely place in which to find fun and laughter. After all, people go there to die, don't they? And isn't it a place where the main focus is pain rather than pleasure, tears rather than smiles, death rather than life? How on earth can you find room for laughing, joking, giggling and smiling in a hospice? Surely caring for someone who is dying is a serious business. Isn't it?"

Sibley answered his own questions when he continued, "Well, my experience has taught me something very important; you can't be serious about death all the time. Humor is often waiting in the wings, ready to leap out at you when you least expect it."

Examples of "waiting in the wings" humor were shared by Sibley through two of his hospice stories. Both are wonderful illustrations of points made throughout this book. The first shows the humor that arises out of the incongruities found in extreme medical situations. The second story gives another example of a patient taking care of the caregiver with humor.

Sid was a wonderful man. He was trying hard to cope with a paralysis that left him highly dependent upon his family and the nurses. This irritated him intensely. But he was also a born actor. He had a wonderful sense of theatre and knew exactly how to act out his sense of injustice in the face of his terminal illness. When Sid was in the mood, he would play to the gallery—in this case three other patients that shared the same room. His roommates tolerated Sid, although "here-he-goes-again" was a much-used refrain amongst themselves.

But Sid was also very religious. One morning, I was giving out the medication in his room when he hoisted himself onto his elbows, looked soulfully across the room and muttered weakly (but loud enough for all to hear) "What day is it today?" I said (quite truthfully) that it was Palm Sunday. Staring up at the ceiling, Sid suddenly blurted out, "Then today is a good day to die." With this he fell back on the bed in such a dramatic fashion that I wondered if he would actually do it then and there!

But a few seconds later he opened his eyes, looked across at me, and sighed.

Later that same week I was back in Sid's room giving out medication once again, and he decided to give a repeat performance. Lifting himself onto his elbows, he looked at me and said, "What day is it today?" Again telling the truth, I said, "It's Good Friday." Just then, from the bed opposite, a fellow patient offered a brilliant punch line. Without looking up from his book he said (as if muttering to himself), "I hope to God he doesn't die today—he might rise again on Sunday!"

Sibley's second story:

When I began working as a nurse in my local hospice over a decade ago I did not expect to be hijacked by humor on my very first day there, but that's what happened.

I was sent to the room of a patient called Bill, who was troubled by chronic constipation, and I was asked to give him an enema. I explained what I was going to do (as if he didn't know!) and waited for his permission to get on with it. Instead I was met with a stony silence. Without taking his eyes from the newspaper he was reading, Bill casually said, "What flavour have you got?" I was startled for a moment but decided to play the game. "Well," I said. "I can do you a blackcurrant or banana flavour— what's it to be?" I had him now! There was a moment of silence whilst he pretended to weigh up the options. Looking me straight in the eye he said, "Let's have two blackcurrant flavoured enemas." "Why two?" I asked. Bill looked at me and winked. "One of them is for you—I hate dining alone!"

Near the end of his letter to me, Sibley said, "I have learned a great deal from the humor of hospice care and I have come to the conclusion that it is wonderful to be mugged by mirth. Laughter can take away some of the fear and the loneliness that so often accompanies the dying process."

Sibley also wrote that Alan Watts, the British-born American philosopher, once said that "the whole art of life is in knowing how to convert anxiety into laughter. If we can learn this in the midst of life, when death comes it may not be so bad after all."

LISTEN FOR LAUGHTER

Although she is a continent away and doesn't know him, Sherry Showalter, a licensed clinical social worker working in a hospice setting, strongly agrees with Sibley. In an article she coauthored, Showalter wrote, "Hospice is about LIFE, about living each day until you die. Humor is about LIFE, a part of living each day until you die."

"At our hospice," Showalter writes, "Tuesday nights are a special time of growth and healing. At 6:30 P.M. people begin to arrive, have a cup of coffee, and share their personal journey of grief. Stories are told, tears are shed and very often the room fills with the sound of laughter—yes, laughter from those who are grieving. We are sure you are wondering," Showalter continues, "what could possibly be funny during a Hospice Bereavement Support Group. The answer is the stories, the struggles, the memories. It is a time of remembering, of growth and healing, and the stories (often sad and painful) have elements of humor just waiting to be acknowledged."

The people in Showalter's support group are not denying the sadness or the pain, but they also are not denying the existence of humor either, humor that at the same time both gives them a respite from their heartache and provides a glimmer of hope to help them get on with their life.

"The work of grief is long and hard," says Showalter, "with part of that work involving learning to laugh again, to speak healing words again." Showalter is of Cherokee heritage. Thus she likes to quote a tribal saying: " 'Listen! Or your tongue will make you deaf.' " To this Showalter adds, "Listening for the humor, the laughter, will empower you to heal, to grow, to restore the balance, and walk in beauty."

QUALITY OF LIFE

For many years, Ron Culberson has been involved with hospice as a licensed clinical social worker and manager. He knows that humor is not only appropriate in hospice work but also necessary: "When dealing with death on a daily basis, it is very easy to lose a perspective on the positive aspects of life. Yet in order to survive, it is crucial to maintain that perspective."

Culberson has learned a few things about humor from his patients. One time, when he was working in home care, one of his patients took a dramatic turn for the worse. "So," he says, "we transferred her to our hospice inpatient facility, which was a very beautiful setting. At one point the woman raised up on her elbows, looked around the room, and told me that she had been 'dying to see this place.' We both laughed heartily at what she said. The woman knew the reality of her situation, otherwise the comment would not have been funny, yet she was able to step back and enjoy her remark." She died six hours later.

This incident taught Culberson that there really is no place that humor is totally absent. "You can find it anywhere. There may be times when it is not appropriate to interject it but it certainly can appear anywhere," says Culberson.

He adds that in hospice care the "quality of life is more important than the amount of life left. It would follow then," he says, "that based on the many studies showing the positive effects of humor on the quality of life, humor and hospice would be a natural fit. So instead of being disrespectful, humor can be a life enhancer even when life is limited."

KEEPING AFLOAT

Patty Wooten worked as a hospice nurse for a number of years. Once Wooten and the pastoral care director, whom she had a very playful rapport with, were feeling overwhelmed after the death of several cherished patients. They sensed that some cheering up might be in order. So Wooten and the director sat down and wrote a song—then sang it, to the tune of "Love and Marriage," as they stepped-kicked, stepped-kicked down the hallway:

> *Grief and Grieving,*
> *Death and Dying.*
> *We are there when folks are crying.*
> *We keep it all together.*
> *'Cause you can't have one without the other.*

When I asked Wooten how there can be so much laughter in hospice work when so many people are dying, she used the analogy of laughter keeping people afloat. "It gives buoyancy so you just don't sink to the bottom. Like a life preserver it helps keep your head above water so you can still breathe. The heaviness of the situation feels like it can pull you under, like you are drowning, and laughter is like a breath of fresh air that you desperately need."

THE GOLDEN CASKET AWARD

Hospice workers use humor not in disrespect but in distancing themselves from tragedy in order to continue to do the work they do. Imagine yourself working in hospice care and attending to *five* different patient deaths within one fourteen-hour night shift. It is hard to conceive this happening, but it does. In fact, several chaplains, social workers, and nurses from the Hospice of Louisville have been in that situation. To acknowledge these dedicated caregivers, and to lift their emotionally exhausted spirits, the hospice presented them with a Golden Casket Award.

This humorous honor comes in the form of a shoe box covered with gold paper. Inside are a small shroud-dressed doll and an assortment of goodies to help the caregiver get through the night. Included are such things as a packet of No-Doz so they won't fall asleep on the job, a Texas catheter so they won't need to stop to go to the bathroom, a high-energy candy bar to feed their body, and a poem to nourish their soul.

While this kind of black humor may seem offensive to a patient or a family, to the hospice caregiver it is a coworker's pat on the back, which playfully says, "I know what you are going through." It is what sustains them and keeps them going.

Death is just a change in lifestyles.

—STEPHEN LEVINE

NO BIG DEAL

The hospice movement has given people a chance for greater participation in the dying process. It is a beginning from which we can question and reevaluate our relationship to life's final moments. We can continue to see humor as a foreign element in dealing with death or we can start to take advantage of all it can offer. The choice is up to us.

An old Chinese proverb states, "You cannot prevent the birds of sorrow from flying overhead, but you can prevent them from making nests in your hair." We don't have to give a home to those birds of sorrow. Humor can help us lighten up our dying and put it in perspective. In *It's Easier Than You Think,* author and meditation teacher Sylvia Boorstein writes about how her father taught her this lesson:

When my father was dying, I remained at his bedside for his final days. The last few days of his life he was primarily in a coma from which he would rouse himself from time to time. We knew he was dying, and we were making him as comfortable as we could, waiting for the last breath. Every once in a while he would seem to breathe his last: his body would shake and he'd have the kind of apnea that people do when they are dying. I would hold his hand and say my prepared speech: "Go to the light" and "Now is your chance to get out of this body." I'm pleased that I did that: those are all the right things to say when someone is dying. ("You've done a good job in this lifetime," "Everybody loved you," "It's time to move on," "You don't need this old body anymore.") Each time he would struggle with the breath, I would give him the speech again. Then he would relax and fall asleep, and I would go back to waiting. Very near the end, he began again a siege of apnea, and I leaped to my feet, beginning my talk about "Go to the light." He opened his eyes, and he looked at me and said quite clearly, "You know, it's not that big of a deal."

ODE TO ELISABETH KÜBLER-ROSS

Like the song quoted earlier in this chapter by Wooten and her hospice pastoral care director, I too wrote a song to lighten up the seriousness of hospice work. Mine is about a pioneer in the death-and-dying movement, Elisabeth Kübler-Ross. It parodies her five stages of dying—denial, anger, depression, bargaining, and acceptance.

Chorus:
Thank you, Elisabeth, for teaching me about dying.
Without you where would I be?
Without you, Elisabeth, I'd be crying trying to die properly.

Your five stages are outrageous.
Your photos of deceased divine.
I'm not afraid of others' dying,
I'm just scared stiff of mine.

Chorus:
So, thank you, Elisabeth, for teaching me about dying.
Without you where would I be?
Without you, Elisabeth, I'd be crying trying to die properly.

You I really do admire,
Teaching me how to expire,
In five easy stages so clear.
I thank you a lots,
Teaching me how to plotz,
And I can do it in less than a year.

I can work on my denial in December,
And anger in April if I remember.
Being depressed in the summer,
Is not such a bummer,
If I can bargain 'til fall leaves appear.

Chorus:
Thank you, Elisabeth, for teaching me about dying.
Without you where would I be?
Without you, Elisabeth, I'd be crying trying to die properly.

Now I know life's just a joke.
I'm ready to croak.
I'll accept acceptance with glory and glee.
But there's one query unsaid—
Before I am dead,
Elisabeth, wouldn't you come with me?

Some of the most rewarding work I have ever done was when I was a hospice volunteer—each and every dying patient taught me something about living. Today, many of the most powerful programs I present are to those who work with the dying or the bereft.

If you are drawn to doing such work, you can contact your local hospice by checking the phone book, contacting your local hospital, or calling the National Hospice Organization, in Arlington, Virginia.

Chapter 7

The C-Words:
Cancer and Comedy

Cancer, schmancer—as long as you're healthy.
—JEWISH SAYING

Putting Cancer
in the Background

Surrounding cancer patients with solemnity when they are already facing possible death does not make sense. It helps neither their current condition nor their recovery. What is needed is something that will aid them in forgetting about cancer. They need something to take their mind off their illness instantly. That something is the other C-word—comedy.

"In truth cancer is a dark disease," says California oncologist William Buchholz, M.D. "It is a life force that has been subverted by all the images that we consider dark. . . . If cancer is a process that is drawing the life force out of people then the way to approach it is through adding lightness to one's life."

Buchholz gave examples of three aspects of *lightening up:* "The most obvious way is a lighter diet since dietary fats contribute to both the initial development of cancer and in some cancers to its perpetuation." According to Buchholz, the second way of achieving lightness, and this is where humor and laughter come in, is "a lighter attitude so you have more enjoyment in life." The final way, says Buchholz, is "lightness in the sense of enlightenment.

This has to do with the insights into one's own life that are needed to be healed.

"My belief, without any data," notes Buchholz, "is that the people who become different from the one in whom the cancer developed are the ones who are more likely to survive. It is as if the cancer comes back, you're not there anymore."

Michael B. Van Scoy–Morsher, M.D., is also an oncologist in California. He says that "one characteristic of the cancer patient who does well is the ability to often put cancer in the background for periods of time."

The examples that follow are from people who, through humor, have managed to achieve a lighter attitude and put cancer in the background for a while.

My reflections on the course of the treatment and the outcome as well as other experiences in treating persons with cancer have caused me to realize that if I want to help them "rejoin the world of the living," I must treat them as though they can still be a part of life. This must, therefore, include the integration of humor into the context of the treatment situation.

—BETTE KISNER

SOMETHING TO FILL ME BACK UP

"Not a day went by that I didn't receive cards, calls, flowers, or meals from family, friends, neighbors, and business associates. But with all the loving gestures of friendship and support, somehow I felt there was something missing. Then it occurred to me. Not once in six months had anyone brought or sent me anything that made me laugh." So says Christine Clifford, author of *Not Now . . . I'm Having a No Hair Day.*

Just once, Clifford says, she wanted someone to bring her something to make her laugh. "I had cried so many tears the well was dry. I needed the tonic and release of laughter. I needed something to fill me back up."

Clifford found that tonic in cartoons—ones she created herself even though she had never drawn cartoons before. Four weeks after the surgery, she says, "I awoke in the middle of the night with a vision: cartoons, as many as 50 of them, popped into my head. For the next several months I worked on my cartoons, often sending them to family and friends to keep their spirits up as I trudged through my treatments."

There are several important points in Clifford's story. Here is another example of a patient who is taking care of friends and family with humor. Here, too, is something I have observed again and again—many people don't know why, but they are drawn toward humor in tough times. On one level, we brush off comedy as being trivial, merely something to make us laugh, but on a deeper, perhaps unconscious level, we know how powerful a good laugh can be.

For Clifford, this call to humor was so strong that it woke her in the middle of the night. Knowing that she needed "something to fill me back up," Clifford found material for comedy everywhere. "Real-life humor was just begging to be picked up and shared," she says.

One time she was going into her daily radiation and passed an elderly man who was coming out of his treatment. As they went by each other, she realized that his pants zipper was down. "So I stopped him," Clifford recalls, "and said, 'Excuse me. I just thought I'd let you know that your fly is open.' " The eighty-something-year-old man looked down, then looked up at Clifford and joked, "Honey, what can't get up, can't get out."

THE CIRCLE THEORY

"I find things funnier than other people do," said Beverly Patterson-Hamilton, a health care educator and cancer patient. "I think that those of us who battle cancer find things funny that other people either don't find funny, or they are afraid to laugh at it, or they are afraid to admit that they find it funny, because it may be insulting."

Hamilton touched upon an important element of humor. I call it my Circle Theory.

Any group of people who are experiencing the same life-challenging adversity (like cancer, AIDS, a major disability, or a disaster) or who are in high-stress jobs (like nurses, firefighters, or policemen) have a common bond. Therefore, they can laugh about things even when the situation itself is not laughable. These people are inside the circle. Others, however—like the families of the seriously ill or those not associated with the high-stress profession—are outside the circle. Not only do those outside the circle usually not see the humor that those inside do, but often they are offended by it.

This is why a cancer patient attending a support group may laugh about some humorous incident within the group, but when they try to explain why they are laughing to someone outside the group, it is not funny.

Hamilton had an excellent example of my Circle Theory. She told me that her sister is HIV-positive. Even though Hamilton was able to joke about her own cancer, she could not laugh about her sister's condition. When her sister joked about losing weight because she was on the Slim-Fast virus, Hamilton was appalled.

The sister was in the HIV circle and found things to laugh about concerning her own health status. Hamilton had difficulty finding anything funny about being HIV-positive because she was outside that circle. She could, however, find humor in her own, cancer world. She shared two of those incidents with me.

Once in an emergency room, when her regular doctor wasn't on call, Hamilton was treated by a different physician. "He barged in," she said, "very cold and very sterile. He looks at my chart and says to me, 'My, you have low blood pressure for someone as large as you are.' So I just bent over him and said, 'Did you know that the number one predictor of a malpractice suit is a poor bedside manner?' " Hamilton said that the nurse had to leave the room because she could not stop laughing.

Another time when Hamilton became ill, she was in the process of getting her doctoral degree. In her usual take-charge manner, she set out to interview oncologists. Below is a conversation that took place between Hamilton and one authoritarian doctor. It reveals Hamilton's wonderful sense of humor and why she is winning her battle with cancer.

> *Doctor:* Well, hello, Bev, how are you today?
> *Hamilton:* I'm fine, Randy.
> *Doctor:* No, I'm Dr. Henderson."
> *Hamilton:* Well, then, I'm Miss Hamilton.
> *Doctor:* I call all my patients by their first name.
> *Hamilton:* I call all my doctors by their first name. So here's the deal. If you call me Bev, I'm calling you Randy. If you call me Beverly, which I prefer, I'm calling you Randall. But if you call me Ms. Patterson-Hamilton, then I'm calling you Dr. Henderson. We are going to do it that way.
> *Doctor:* But I'm a doctor. I went to med school.
> *Hamilton:* It doesn't mean you're smarter than me. It just means you got started before I did. Now, how are we going to handle this?

The doctor was taken aback; Hamilton thought the whole thing was rather humorous. "We finally settled," she says, "on *Randall* and *Beverly.*"

But that's not all to the story. About eight months after the incident the doctor told Hamilton that their encounter had infuriated him so much that he went and talked to several other oncologists about it. They thought it was hysterically funny. Moreover, because of Hamilton's tenaciousness, one of the other oncologists remarked, "That woman is going to live. That woman is going to make it."

The Comedic
Accoutrements of Cancer

In the shower I reached up and a huge clump of hair came out in my hand. Then another. I didn't mind at all. I got Ken and we both stood in front of the mirror, looking at each other, both completely bald. What a sight! "My god," Ken said, "we look like the melon section in a supermarket. Promise me one thing: we'll never go bowling."

—TREYA KILLAM WILBER, IN KEN WILBER, *Grace and Grit*

Where does humor come from when someone has cancer and there is a threat that their life may be limited? Patients frequently find something to laugh about in such things as their chemo-produced baldness, the wigs they use to cover up baldness, prosthetic devices, and even nipple substitutes.

CANCER HAIR

Forty thousand women a year die of breast cancer. JoAnn Loulan's mother was one of them. JoAnn lived in fear of getting cancer too, and she did. In the following piece, from her forthcoming book, Loulan writes humorously about her cancer. She notes that some people may take offense at her writing about cancer in this way because, in her own words, "how can cancer possibly be fun? But of course that's the point," she says; "it really isn't any fun." Loulan, who claims to have a major investment in her self-proclaimed "big hair," exaggerates losing it to find some fun anyway.

> After worrying about dying, I worried about my hair. I worried that it would fall out in clumps with one of the treatments. I worried that it would go straight. I worried that it would change texture. I worried that I would go bald. I worried that I was so worried about it. I worried that it was so shallow of me. I worried that cancer, among other things, had made me superficial.
>
> I thought it was supposed to do the opposite. I thought it

was supposed to make me deep and sage. I thought it was supposed to make me contemplative and knowing. I thought cancer would make me want to do good deeds. I thought it would help me learn to spell easily and be able to do math and clean out my refrigerator. I thought it would reorient my priorities. I thought I would work less, play more.

Mostly what happened is that I thought people would see my hair and know I was a cancer patient. They would walk by, like I had to hundreds of strangers in my life, and feel pity all because of seeing hair that looked like it was "Cancer Hair." Cancer Hair, a new style. One worn by other members of the clan—Chihuahuas, possums, dogs with mange, rats of various descriptions. None flattering I can tell you. Only pot belly pigs emerge from the cancer inspired hair style looking extremely cute. Really no other living thing looks cute with Cancer Hair. Everyone knows that no matter what they tell you.

BUDDHA WITHOUT THE WISDOM

In the January 1993 edition of *McCall's,* TV journalist Linda Ellerbee wrote about some of her cancer experiences and of being bald:

> I'm not suggesting laughing at other people's miseries, but you can certainly laugh at your own. If you don't, you have to find other ways to survive, and they all sound a lot harder than laughing.
>
> Looking for the humor in things is a skill that has gotten me through even the worst of situations. In 1992, I discovered I had breast cancer and needed a double mastectomy. Cancer is serious. But there are funny things about it too.
>
> That summer I bought some breast prostheses to use while swimming. Instead of fastening them to my skin with Velcro as the directions instructed, I simply inserted the prostheses into my bathing suit. When I came out of the water, one had migrated around to my back! Now, how can you not laugh at such a thing? Either you laugh or you cry your eyes out.
>
> Sometimes you have to give others permission to laugh with—or even at—you. When a friend went with me to buy a wig to cover my hair loss from chemotherapy, we giggled at

some of the truly silly-looking wigs we saw. Upset, the sales-woman said to my friend, "You shouldn't be laughing. Your friend has cancer. This is serious." I said, "No, you don't understand. A wig is not serious." And she said smiling, "You know, you're right."

It's something I've tried to teach my kids as well. When my 23-year-old daughter saw me with my bald head and no breast, she said, "You look just like a Buddha without the wisdom," and we both howled. I think we are never braver than when we stand tall and look into the sun and laugh. Laughter may be a form of courage.

....

Upon my otherwise billiard-bald head remained two discreetly placed corkscrew tufts, one by each ear. They looked exactly like payess, the long sideburns worn by Hasidic Jewish men. My choices were clear: I could enter the yeshiva or buy a wig. But first, some scarves, some hats, some immediate cover, since the wig I wanted—hand-sewn human hair—would take at least a couple of weeks.

Meanwhile, my yeshiva hair came in real handy. With those little wisps hanging out of my favorite floppy khaki hat (plus makeup, sunglasses and giant earrings) no one even knew I was bald. No one even knew I was me. And when those little wisps hung out of my brilliantly tied Moroccan scarf—with several deco floral-patterned scarves, time-consumingly* french-braided and swirled around same—strangers were literally stopping me on the street to ask how to duplicate my "statement."

—FANNY GAYNES, *How Am I Gonna Find a Man If I'm Dead?*

*Once, late for a supper party, I explained to my hosts, "I just washed my scarves and couldn't do a thing with them."

....

NIPPLES IN THE NIGHT

As we saw in the hospital chapter, humor often arises out of absurdity. The comedy of cancer is no different. Things get so nonsensical that we can do nothing but laugh. Such is the case in the following two stories.

After her mastectomy, author Betty Rollin had trouble locating made-to-order prosthetic breasts. She did, however, find ready-made ones, but to her surprise, none came with a nipple. In *First, You Cry,* Rolling turns the ludicrousness of the situation into laughter. She writes:

Swell, I thought. Wonderful. I was an outcast in the land of out-casts. I was not only a one-titted woman in a two-titted world. I was an erect-nippled one-titted woman in a flat-nippled one-titted world. . . .

I called Reach for Recovery. Yes, they knew of a made-to-order place. In California. I called the man in California. Yes, he did make nipples. Yes, his "forms," as he called them, did have to be worn inside a bra, and yes, he would send me a brochure.

The problem was I had begun to do on-camera work again during the day; we were going out more at night. I felt that I could not go one more day without a nipple. Whereupon it occurred to me that perhaps I could make one myself—attach something small and pointed to the nylon cover of the Dacron wad. I headed for my sewing box, rummaged through spools of thread, buttons, pincushions, and cards of needles and pins, and there, in one corner of the box, under a green button, was a black nipple. Actually, it was a black cloth cuff link. But I knew right away it would work. I pulled up my blouse and held it next to my right nipple. Perfect. That is, the size and shape were perfect. The color, black, was not perfect. But what the hell. I wasn't planning to wear any see-through blouses.

Just as I threaded a needle and went to work, Arthur came home. "What are you doing?" he said.

"I just invented a nipple and I'm sewing it on," I said. "Now I know how Eli Whitney felt."

Like Rollin, humorist Lola Gillebaard too had trouble locating a nipple. After her reconstructive breast surgery, Gillebaard went shopping for one, but she got more than she bargained for. Gillebaard explains:

One night after work, I went to this place. There was nobody there but one man. So I walked up to him, looked him right in the eye and said, "I need a nipple." He said, "I beg your pardon." I said, "Look, I just had reconstruction and I'm looking to top it off with a nipple."

Then the man behind the counter said, "The two ladies who run that department have gone to a mastectomy convention."

"Fine," I said, "but I still need a nipple."

The man threw his hands up and said, "Look, I don't know

where it is but if you want to help me look I know it's here someplace."

"Okay," I said, "let's get started."

We opened just about every box around. I saw things, I had no idea what they were. And Lord knows, I hope I never find out! But in the end we never did locate a nipple. So, disappointed, I went home "nippleless."

The next morning one of the sales ladies called to apologize. The sales clerk said, "Please come back. I know right where they are."

"Well," I responded, "why don't you tell that man."

So I went back and bought two nipples. One for show and one for stow.

And they worked beautifully. They looked just like a pastie. The only thing was, it only had one position. It looked like I was turned on all the time.

One night after Gillebaard got her nipple, she woke screaming, "There's a bug on my back! There's a bug on my back!" Her husband, Hank, swatted it and declared, "Honey, I got it." Then he turned on the light, threw the bug on the floor, and began to stomp up and down on it while yelling, "It's dead. I know it's dead."

"Do you want to see it?" Hank asked his wife. "No," she responded, "I don't want to see it." But Hank insisted.

He then handed her what was left of her nipple.

"I was glad I bought one to stow," Gillebaard declares.

....

As I left the doctor's office the nurse put an envelope in my hand and said, "This isn't a real prosthesis, but slip it into your bra and you'll look a little more balanced." In the car, I opened the envelope, extracted a small wad of cotton, and shouted, "My God! I've got bigger dust balls under my bed than this!"

—ERMA BOMBECK

....

NO NOSE

In my humor programs, I do an exercise with red clown noses. Everyone in the audience gets a sealed packet with one inside. With their eyes closed, I ask them to think of some problem, worry, or stress they are having and then, still with their eyes closed, to open the packet and put the clown nose on. Then I ask the audience to open their eyes and look around the room. There are often gales of laughter as everyone in the room—and often this means hundreds of people—has clown noses on.

I was a little reluctant to do this activity, however, when I addressed the annual meeting of the National Coalition of Cancer Survivorship. I knew that a number of people in the group had facial cancer. Some had only a partial nose, some none at all.

I checked with the meeting planner to make sure that the clown-nose process was appropriate. She assured me that even those with facial disfigurement would love it. Still, I was uncomfortable about doing it. My fears were quickly alleviated, however, when the group not only responded with overwhelming laughter but also delighted in sharing stories with me about their prosthetic noses.

One woman joyfully showed me a Polaroid photo taken in her hotel room minutes before my speech. She told me that she was getting ready to attend my talk and proceeded to put adhesive glue on her prosthetic nose. Then she waited for it to dry. When it came time to attach the nose, however, it was gone. She could not find it.

Just then, a friend knocked on the door to remind her that it was time to go hear my program. But still no nose. So she asked her friend to help her locate it. That's when the picture was taken. Her friend had found her nose. There it was, stuck to her rear end.

She delighted in telling me the story and in explaining the photo. But she was even more elated with her new clown nose. She said, "This is great. From now on, I have a choice of which nose to wear."

Of course serious illness is serious! Why else would they call it "serious?" That is all the more reason to avail yourself of every advantage—including laughter.

—RONNA FAY JEVNE AND ALEXANDER LEVITAN,
No Time for Nonsense

Finding Joy

Undoubtedly, it is sad to see a friend or loved one near death. But that doesn't mean we can't create a moment or two of joy within those dark times—a few bright moments that might be remembered long after the person is gone.

Several years ago, for example, there was a story in *People* magazine about a man with cancer. He had had chemotherapy and lost all of his hair. To offer some lighthearted support, three friends came to the hospital with their heads shaved. When the man came home from the hospital, dozens of people in his neighborhood shaved their heads too.

We can't all go around shaving our heads all the time, but we can—as with the private violin concert mentioned in the hospice chapter—creatively seek ways to bring some joy into someone's final days. Here are two examples of how people created some joy in the dying process, the first by some friends, the second by the patient herself.

DANCING ELEPHANTS

Rita Derbas, a colleague from northern California, told me this story about creating a special event for a dying friend:

> Like the movie *Four Seasons,* with Alan Alda, we had a bunch of couples who did everything together—especially vacations. One member, Roger, was skiing with us one week, and a month later he was diagnosed with lung cancer. Needless to say, it was a shock to all of us since Roger never smoked, was an avid diver and a wonderful singer.
>
> We all took very special care of Roger, taking turns visiting him, bringing him his favorite foods, and rubbing his feet.
>
> As he failed, a friend asked, "Roger, is there anything you want?" He replied, "Nothing really, except maybe a dancing elephant."
>
> It was Roger's wish and we were going to make it happen.
>
> As true friends, we rallied the group, made "We love you, Roger" signs, and waited to surprise him. At the appointed time, an ambulance took an unknowing Roger to a helicopter pad area, then wheeled him out to waving signs—and a real live elephant. He was surprised, overwhelmed, and very much loved.
>
> So how did we arrange for an elephant to be at an appointed location at an appointed time? First, we called Marine World Africa, U.S.A. They referred us to a trainer who free-

lanced one of the elephants. His business, would you believe, is named Elephants R Us. The elephant came down in a huge trailer. She stood up on two legs, danced, and hugged Roger. So, believe or not, there is a business that rents elephants out for special occasions—and this was a *very* special occasion.

One final note—Roger often wore red socks; it was kind of a trademark of his. So now, when we feel the pangs of Roger's loss, we all put on red socks and remember the dancing elephant.

DANCING INTO LIFE . . . AND DEATH

Betsy Morscher and I met six years ago at a National Speakers Association conference. She was an international health spa consultant and a nationally known speaker. I was first attracted to her because of the bright colors she was wearing, which perfectly matched her bubbly and colorful personality. Near the end of our conversation, we signed each other's dance card and agreed to dance together that evening at the awards banquet.

As it turned out, instead of one dance, we danced nearly all. We danced at every convention and winter workshop following that too. That is, until Betsy was diagnosed with ovarian cancer. I lost a dance partner but I gained a wealth of wisdom on how one can dance through life, and death . . . and never miss a beat.

When she was ailing, every Thursday night Betsy would invite friends into her home for a "laff-in." They told jokes and funny stories and sang songs. Sometimes a professional stand-up comedian would join the group. Once a clown came by and brought along some costumes for everyone to wear. Men used balloons for boobs; women had funny wigs and animal noses on; all were part of Betsy's plan to focus on life rather than on death.

Betsy asked friends to help her find humor, but she also was good at creating it herself. She, for example, nicknamed her oxygen tank Otto. When Betsy was invited somewhere, she was frequently heard saying, "Otto and I would be glad to come." On special occasions, Otto the oxygen tank was emblazoned with a big pink bow.

Otto even attended Betsy's dance class three times a week and became her regular dance partner. If Otto ever became unavailable, Betsy declared she would put a wig on her I.V. pole and dance with it.

But Betsy's search for humor wasn't only for the sake of laughing. As her daughter, Maria, explains, "There was always the light part of humor, but it also led to a deeper connection." One time Betsy invited friends to crawl in bed with her and asked them to tell her what she meant to them and what they had learned from her. "Things would get serious for a while," notes Maria, "and then somebody would say or do something silly and the laughter would begin again."

I know that cancer often kills,
But so do cars and sleeping pills;
And it can hurt one till one sweats,
So can bad teeth and unpaid debts.
A spot of laughter, I am sure,
Often accelerates one's cure;
So let us patients do our bit
To help the surgeons make us fit.
—J.B.S. HALDANE,
"CANCER'S A FUNNY THING"

Creatively Conquering Cancer

Amazingly, some cancer patients have been able to turn their illness into entertainment. Using their creative juices, they have found comedy in cancer through such art forms as poetry, theatrical performances, and even stand-up comedy routines.

DOCTORS ARE . . .

In *It's Always Something*, comedian Gilda Radner wrote, "Cancer is probably the most unfunny thing in the world, but I'm a comedienne, and even cancer couldn't stop me from seeing humor in what I went through. . . . I have a theory now that cancer cells hate laughter and jokes and songs and dancing. They want to leave when too much of that is going on. They love gloom and depression and sadness and fear, but joy makes them want to move out."

In order to keep those cancer cells at bay, and get an upper hand on an illness that has knocked them down, a number of cancer patients have turned to humorous poetry. Radner, for example, wrote the following poem, which appeared in the *New England Journal of Medicine*:

Doctors are whippersnappers in ironed white coats,
Who spy up your rectums and look down your throats,
And press you and poke you with sterilized tools,
And stab at solutions that pacify fools.
I used to revere them and do what they said,
'Til I learned what they learned on was already dead.

NIGHTLY RITUAL

In her self-published book, Janet Henry's poems poke fun at every aspect of cancer. Here is one from *Surviving the Cure: . . . A Time to Laugh:*

I prop up my wig on the dresser
And tuck my prosthesis beneath,
And thank God I still go to bed with
My man and my very own teeth.

SUMMARY

"I was diagnosed with Stage III cancer in April of 1992," states Barbara Whipple. "At the time," she continues, "I was thirty-eight, married, and the mother of a four-year-old girl. After a mastectomy uncovered a tumor the size of a baseball and five positive lymph nodes, I had aggressive chemotherapy, a bone marrow transplant, and a few other related minor surgeries. But I'm still here. I'm in remission. I survived it."

Not only did Whipple survive, but she sometimes even found humor in her ordeal. Being a poet, she naturally used the medium of poetry to express her feelings about having cancer. Her self-published book *I've Got Cancer, but It Doesn't Have Me!* contains several lighthearted cancer-related poems. Whipple says she focuses on the lighter side of her illness because "what's the point of living if you are not going to enjoy it?"

I think back over all that happened
and know that it wasn't always that sad
that there is humor in anything
if you're willing to see it.

Before I went into the hospital
I only had a few sprigs of hair left
but my long-time hairdresser couldn't bring herself
to shave my head
so I went to the local barbershop instead
plopped down in the chair
lifted off my wig
and said
"just take it off the top"
which he did without a blink
as the eyes of the old men peered over
the tops of their newspapers
and tried not to stare.
And later when the other social workers
from work came by for a visit
I drove crazy Carl's phallic hot red Corvette
roaring around the streets
of the winding small town
without my wig on
as people gaped and took a second glance
at my shiny bald head and lipstick laughter flying by.
Sometimes I would say to people who
didn't know me well, "You want to see something?"
and then I'd lift my wig off
and for a moment they'd look around
to see if they were on Candid Camera.
And once I tossed my prosthesis to a friend
to hold so I could roll down a grassy hill
out in the country on a sublime summer's day.
Cancer has taught me to be spontaneous
to be more playful
more bold and daring
it has allowed me to live in the moment
and to do what I want
to be whoever I want to be
however I feel
a freedom that very few people have
and yet yearn for
a luxury I would never give up.

Someone asked, "Did you have colon cancer?" and I said, "Well, mine was a little bit different; I had cancer of the semi-colon."

—STEVE ALLEN

GOD SAID, "HA!"

Former *Saturday Night Live* cast member Julia Sweeney experienced three major setbacks in one year—divorce, the death of her brother, and her own serious illness. In spite of the triple blow, Sweeney turned her misfortunes into a comic monologue. It covers the period when her brother, who was dying of cancer, moved in with her, when her parents followed to take care of him, and when she underwent a radical hysterectomy.

Sweeney dealt with all of this not-so-funny stuff by finding the humor in it. Weekly she would go down to the local comedy club, the Uncabaret, and do a routine about what was going on in her life. That material became her book and her one-woman Broadway show, *God Said, "HA!"*

In both the book and the show, Sweeney talks about the funny things that happened between her and her brother. "When I told Mike I had cancer, he said, 'You just couldn't stand it, could you? An actress not being in the cancer spotlight." Mike, according to Sweeney, kept his sense of humor to the end. After they were both diagnosed, the two siblings would mischievously answer the phone, "Hello! House of Cancer."

After her brother died, she continued to go back to the Uncabaret to talk about the "surreal moments" of her own illness. For instance: "At one point, the doctors told me they seemed to have lost my ovaries. I go, 'Excuse me? Am I going to, like cough one up or something?'" And: "The doctors said I could still have kids if I have the eggs fertilized in vitro and then find a surrogate. I go, 'Oh, great. Now I have to meet a guy *and* a girl."

One of the worst moments, recalls Sweeney, and one of the funniest as well, occurred in the hospital. She explains: "One day I'm in the bathroom with the door closed and my mom is outside the door. She goes, 'Did you go yet?' I say, 'Yes.' She goes, 'Good girl!' and starts clapping."

Finding comedy in the catastrophic circumstances she went through doesn't mean it was all a barrel of laughs when she performed onstage.

One reporter, for example, asked, "Was there ever a time . . . when all of a sudden everything that you managed to find to laugh at slipped away and you were left with the tragedy of it all?"

Sweeney replied, "Oh, yeah. In fact, while I was writing it [*God Said,*

"HA!"], it was never as tragic and difficult as certain moments of performing it . . . there would be always a different moment in the show where I didn't know if I could go on."

"But you do," interjects the interviewer.

"But I do," says Sweeney.

FROM SURVIVING TO THRIVING

Jane Hill, of Santa Ana, California, is a wife, mother, and stand-up comedian. She is also a breast cancer survivor. After having five surgeries, she now shares her humor with audiences in order to help them not only survive but also, as she does, thrive.

Instead of calling her operation a mastectomy, she tells people, "I prefer to call it a breast reduction operation. After all, they did reduce two to one!" Hill says locating a business suit is also a major problem. She can't find "any with a single-breasted jacket," and "after wearing a size thirty-four bra all those years, I now have trouble finding a size seventeen."

After her many surgeries, Hill, who compares her operations to airline travel, says she thought she had enough "frequent gurney miles" for a free operation. But not quite—only enough miles for a one-way ticket. "But," she says jokingly, "if I can schedule my next surgery between June and September, with an overnight stay on Saturday, I'll get enough bonus miles not only for my next operation, but I can also take a companion along for free."

Continuing her routine, Hill asks her audience, who are frequently cancer survivors, "How many of you went for a second opinion for your condition?" After most of the audience raises their hands, Hill shares, "I did too after they told me I had cancer—of the prostrate!"

Hill ends her routine by reminding audiences to "keep laughing to keep healthy." She also tells them to look for her new television series—*The Young and the Breastless.*

SEEDS OF THE BEST

The awareness that death may be approaching faster than we thought it would can make us more aware of life. Joe Kogel, a sportswriter-turned-performance-artist, for example, has developed a one-man show dealing with the trials and tribulations of living with malignant melanoma. It is called *Life and Death: Very Funny Stories About Very Scary Things.* In it Kogel relates how being diagnosed with cancer at the age of twenty-five was one of the best things that ever happened to him. He says he "felt more in the five days after his diagnosis than in the previous twenty-five years."

It is probably hard for people who have not gone through this experience to understand how anything as devastating as a cancer prognosis—or any other life-challenging illness, for that matter—can be uplifting. However, when time is limited, frequently we try to make it of a higher quality. Anyone who has ever been in therapy, for example, knows that the last ten minutes of a session often accomplishes more than the previous fifty.

According to Kogel, the bottom line is simply this: "An appreciation of the preciousness of life could be a means of living more gracefully [and] . . . dying more gracefully whenever that time comes, be it as a result of cancer or the Number 52 bus running over you in the middle of an otherwise harmless Thursday afternoon."

Kogel has tried to make his entire life more meaningful since his diagnosis by sharing his insights about having cancer in a humorous and entertaining way. For example:

> I saw my mother stuffing the cosmic ballot box with her prayers, as though she were scribbling "Save Joe Kogel" on thousands of tiny scraps of paper and sending them up to God. Each morning, God wakes up, puts on the coffee, and sits down to open the morning prayers. First slip of paper: "Save Joe Kogel." Second slip: "Save Joe Kogel." Third slip: "Save . . . Joe Kogel." So God asks his secretary, "Say, who is this Kogel guy anyway?"

This Joe Kogel is a someone who has found the comedy in cancer. In his show, he reminds his audiences of what he calls the Kogel Effect—"The worst thing in your life," he says, "may contain the seeds of the best."

KEEPING 'EM IN STITCHES

Others, with perhaps less performance skills than Sweeney, Hill, or Kogel, have come up with their own wonderfully creative devices for looking at the lighter side of cancer.

One young woman, for example, who was diagnosed with uterine cancer, designed and sent out invitations to a "coming-out party" for her upcoming hysterectomy.

She told guests that festivities would include "unfertility rites," "a menstrual cycle race," and an "auction of miscellaneous contraceptive paraphernalia." She also poked fun at her four-week forced abstinence from sexual intercourse and asked friends to guess how many tumors would be found (the "fibroid pool").

In addition, she encouraged people to visit her by telling them that there would be "plenty of womb for everybody." But she informed them not to send or bring anything too funny during the first few days after the operation, because, she said, "I'll already be in stitches."

A ROOM WITH A VIEW

In Dr. Rachel Naomi Remen's wonderful book *Kitchen Table Wisdom,* she writes about one woman who used her creativity to make one weekend extraordinarily special:

> After completing the last treatment in a year of potent chemotherapy one of my clients went to San Francisco overnight with her husband to celebrate. Her oncologist had tried to discourage her from this ... but she and her husband had gone anyway and stayed in a nice hotel.
>
> Afterwards, I asked her about it. "It was wonderful," she said. "First, we ordered room service. They brought it in on a table with a cloth a half-inch thick. My first meal without a tray. It was so elegant, the wineglasses and the butter carved into little flowers. And the food! We sat in this lovely room overlooking a little park and ate real food that I could actually taste. In the nude. Then we made love. Then we took long, long hot baths and used up every single towel in the bathroom. Great big thick towels—there were twelve of them. And we used up all those delicious-smelling things in the little bottles. And watched both movies. And ate most of what was in the little refrigerator. And sat outside on the terrace in our bathrobes and saw the moon rise over the city. We found all the pillows that they hid in the dresser drawers and slept in this king-size bed with eight pillows. And saw the sunrise. We used it all up. It was glorious!" she said to me, a woman who spends most of the time in a hotel room asleep.

We who have terminal ailments should simply work at making ourselves happy, if indeed that should be called work, and let the doctors take care of the rest.

—ED MADDEN, *Carpe Diem*

CANCER BECOMES ME

No, humor alone can't change a cancer diagnosis, but what it can do is make sure your mental anguish is less agonizing.

The final selection in this chapter, by Marjorie Gross, does exactly that. With tongue in cheek, her writing, originally published in the *New Yorker,* sarcastically pokes fun at various aspects of cancer. In the end, Gross even finds some humorous benefits in having the disease.

On being diagnosed:

What really happens is the doctor walks in and gives you the sympathetic head tilt that right away tells you, "Don't buy in bulk." The degree of tilt corresponds directly with the level of bad news. You know, a little tilt: "We've caught it in time"; sixty-degree angle: "Spread to the lymph nodes"; forty-five-degree angle: "Spread to your clothes."

On alternative cancer treatments:

Then, there are my other friends, who are bugging me to go alternative. So now I'm inundated with articles, books, and pamphlets on healers, nutritionists, and visualization. . . . I was also given a crystal by a friend who was going through a messy divorce. She was given the crystal by a guy who died of AIDS. As far as I was concerned, this crystal had a terrible résumé. As far as the healing power of crystals goes, let me just say that I grew up eating dinner under a crystal chandelier every night, and look what came of *that:* two cancers, a busted marriage, and an autistic little brother. There, the healing power of crystals. Enjoy.

The cancer advantage:

I hope with all this negative talk I haven't painted too bleak a picture and therefore discouraged you from getting cancer. I mean, there are some really good things about it. Like:

1. You automatically get called courageous. The rest of you people have to save somebody from drowning. We just have to wake up.

2. You are never called rude again. You can cancel appointments left and right, leave boring dinners after ten minutes, and still not become a social pariah.

3. Everyone returns your calls immediately. . . .

4. People don't ask you to help them move.

5. If you're really shameless, you never have to wait in line for anything again. Take off the hat and get whisked to the front.

So it hasn't been all bad.

MUCH OF IT IS FUNNY

To conclude this chapter, we turn to Anatole Broyard's brilliant book *Intoxicated by My Illness*. In it he writes eloquently about the final months of his life after he was diagnosed with prostate cancer. One of the striking points he makes is that "illness is primarily a drama, and it should be possible to enjoy it as well as to suffer it. . . . Illness," after all, "is not all tragedy. Much of it is funny."

As we have seen in the preceding stories about cancer, much of it *is* laughable.

Chapter 8

AIDS Ain't Funny
—or Is It?

The threat of dying ought to make people witty, since they
are already concentrated.

—ANATOLE BROYARD,
Intoxicated by My Illness

All Its Garish Colors

"A critical illness," Broyard writes, "is like a great permission, an authorization or absolving. It's all right for a threatened man to be romantic, even crazy, if he feels like it. All your life," he continues, "you think you have to hold back your craziness, but when you're sick you can let it out in all its garish colors."

While Broyard did not have acquired immune deficiency syndrome, he could very well have been writing about the gay and lesbian community, who have been hit hardest with this disease. For they have been letting out all their garish and glorious colors for years by using humor as a weapon against their oppressors. They courageously continue to do so against their most recent and devastating enemy, AIDS.

I have had numerous friends and colleagues who either have been diagnosed with AIDS or are HIV-positive. I've noticed that after the shock of their diagnosis wore off, many of them found that their life seemed fuller, richer, and, yes, sometimes even sprinkled with humor.

Indeed, AIDS is a horrendous pandemic. Many people with this disease will face a miserable death. One grief counselor felt that AIDS was much worse than a bad cancer death. "It's sadder because of the deterioration and the fact that people die a lot younger than in many other diseases. (The average age group is twenty-two to forty-four). You have young people who are blind, who can't walk, and who are disfigured with scars. So it is harder to find humor when things are that bad."

For these reasons, and also because people with AIDS may be closeted and therefore less willing to speak out than, say, people with other life-threatening illnesses, humorous stories about AIDS are indeed harder to come by. The fact that at the time of this writing AIDS has killed over three hundred thousand people in the United States is certainly not funny. Yet there are funny things about this disease. The stories that follow prove that.

Something to Laugh About

It simply makes sense to try to mobilize whatever immune-enhancing effects might flow from marshaling the mind. After all, even if your T-cells don't increase, how can having a cheerful, frisky, life-affirming attitude possibly hurt? . . . I highly recommend daily doses of laughter.

—MICHAEL CALLEN, long-term AIDS survivor

DO THEY SHOW
MARY TYLER MOORE RERUNS?

Howard Shapiro is one of the three hundred thousand people who have died of AIDS in this country. Before his death, he wrote a monthly column for *The Body Positive,* a New York–based newsletter/magazine geared toward people who are HIV-positive. During his three-year stint, his byline changed from Howard Shapiro to Howard Aaron Shapiro, but it almost didn't matter, because everyone knew him by the name of his column, "Kvetch"—a wonderful Yiddish word meaning "to complain persistently."

Like many Yiddish words, however, *kvetch* has a more colorful meaning than simply complaining. Someone who kvetches does so, not so much in order to get things corrected or fixed, but to complain for the sake of complaining. In fact, someone who kvetches does so to the point of being ludicrous.

In his columns, Kvetch (aka Howard Shapiro, aka Howard Aaron

Shapiro) humorously wrote about, and kvetched about, such things as dating in the age of AIDS, alternative healings, medications, hospital visits, disability insurance, and his continuing courtship of celebrities for his cause.

Kvetching? Perhaps. Ludicrous? Yes. Laughable? Without a doubt.

One day from Kvetch's "The Jewish Journals":

This fat nurse with sideburns forced Kvetch to breathe into a saline solution. First you cough, then you gag and spit up in a jar. So much for privacy. All the patients watched me perform this glamorous act like it was dinner theater. The paramedic applauded and a wheelchair bound man gave me a standing ovation. I've been booked for a return engagement in ICU. I'll be starring in *Funny Girl*.

Two days from the "Kvetch Kronicles":

Tuesday—Meals on Wheels delivered four frozen chicken dinners to my apartment and had the nerve to try and take them back a half an hour later after they realized they had the wrong sick person. The embarrassing thing is that I had already sold the meals to some old ladies in the laundry room at $10.00 a pop.

Friday—Broadway star and professional coffee drinker Carol Lawrence personally called me and applauded my comic talents and dubbed me—"an AIDS humorist." I told her living with AIDS couldn't be as bad as living with Robert Goulet!

Kvetch on alternative healing:

In the last couple of weeks I have been detoxifying all over NYC since starting a holistic approach to HIV. WARNING: I would not try this method of healing without the advice of a medical doctor, nutritionist, psychic healer or exorcist! The things that have been coming out of my body (a 1969 Pontiac Firebird, moon rocks, my Hebrew school report card, and an album of *Patty Duke's Greatest Hits*) would shock an electrician.

Kvetch once wrote, "I'm a joker," and indeed he was. Even his final column, which talked about his hatred of AIDS, allowed Kvetch to both curse his disease and be comic about it at the same time.

The angel flew into my open window like Peter Pan. He could have called first. My angel is beautiful. He wears leather chaps, a Donna Karan jacket and a toupee under his halo. He wanted to take me for a ride on his wings. "Before I go," I said, "I have some questions for you."

1. Does heaven have *TV Guide*?
2. How's the pizza?
3. Do you have to do the dishes?
4. Can you have candy before dinner?
5. Do they show "Mary Tyler Moore" reruns?

I believe God is always there with us in our hearts and our minds. He may come to us in the shape of many things, a smile, a sunrise, a kind word, or an understanding look. He may come to us disguised as a hilarious joke or the ability to laugh at ourselves and our situation in our most desperate hours.

—CHER

I HEAL UP SCAR

On the other side of the country, another newsletter, *Positive Living*, is published by AIDS Project, Los Angeles. It, like *The Body Positive*, contains a monthly column that frequently looks at the lighter side of HIV and AIDS.

Like Howard Shapiro's "Kvetch" columns, Paul Serchia's "Thinking Positive" column often uses a common comedic technique, exaggeration, to achieve a humorous perspective on a not-so-funny disease.

In one column, for example, Serchia wrote an exaggerated to-do list. Here are a few things on his schedule:

• Remove Dr. Kevorkian from my Christmas card list.
• Stop pestering Sunset Books to publish a how-to manual on casket building.
• Prepare for a mid-life crisis—in case I live long enough to have one.
• Panic about retirement.
• Just for the hell of it, get a five-year subscription to MAD.
• Get Forest Lawn to return my deposit on that plot I've had my eye on.

In another column, Serchia humorously exaggerates things people who don't have AIDS might say to those who do:

"Let's take your car. You have the handicapped permit."

"You look different somehow. Is that lesion new?"

"I brought *Schindler's List, Philadelphia* and *Longtime Companion.* I thought watching movies would cheer you up."

In my half-day and all-day humor programs, I frequently do a process in which the audience looks at how a child might playfully deal with a stressful adult event. Generally, only a few of the ideas generated are practical; adults, after all, cannot do some of the antics kids concoct. In spite of this, the process is very valuable. As the participants discuss the absurd and often silly things kids might do to solve adult problems, the workshop attendees quickly discover that they are laughing, and in doing so get a new perspective on the things that stress them out.

Serchia frequently uses play in his columns to find the laughter too. One column, for example, used the wordplay game of anagrams to come up with some daffy definitions of AIDS-related items. (An anagram is the re-arranging of the letters of one word to form another word or phrase.)

> • It is my theory that pharmaceutical companies get a giggle out of camouflaging the true content of their products inside of their wacky trademark names. Consider *Retrovir:* RIVER ROT.
> • Studying names of institutions often exposes their embarrassing function. Take *Food and Drug Administration:* TRINITARIANS FUND DODO DOGMA.
> • So the next time AIDS befuddlement sets in, look at things in a new way. It works. Or my name is not . . . I HEAL UP SCAR. [Which cleverly is an anagram for its author, Paul Serchia.]

Serchia knows that he cannot cure his illness by simply using wordplay or exaggeration, but he also knows that, as it does for the participants in my workshops, humor can give him a new outlook toward his disease. If he can laugh about something, he has something to live for.

> As another anniversary of my HIV diagnosis approaches this fall, I have begun to notice that my outlook on the future is improving. Some benchmarks:
> I booked airline reservations for myself for travel back East for a 10-day vacation at the end of May. It's a round-trip ticket. And I didn't even ask the travel agent if there would be a surcharge if on the return trip I was loaded in a box as cargo . . .

[and] certain groceries, I am proud to say, I now purchase in bulk quantities. A dozen eggs. What a dramatic concept.

Humor Is Vital

Did you hear the joke about an AIDS patient who said, "In my condition, I don't even buy green bananas anymore."

You may not think that this is funny. You may even think that it is in poor taste. And if you are not living with AIDS, or are HIV-positive, you may be right. But this joke comes from a man with acquired immune deficiency syndrome. "AIDS," says stand-up comedian Mark Johnson, "is a heavy trip and we all need a break from it. Humor is a great way to do that. Some people may be offended that we can laugh about the subject, but it really helps sometimes."

If nothing else, laughter brings those with AIDS closer together while making things more tolerable. At one social gathering, for example, seven beepers went off moments apart, reminding their owners that it was time to take their medication. "No one could figure out if it was their beeper or someone else's," said group member. "We all had to laugh. Sometimes finding a humorous side to something so tragic makes it a little bit more bearable."

Steve Moore is another stand-up comedian. He is also HIV-positive. Moore has played at some of the most prestigious comedy clubs across America and has headlined with such celebrities as Dolly Parton and Joan Rivers. He uses comedy both to entertain and to educate his mostly straight audiences. He says, "It can get very quiet sometimes when I'm playing a straight club. If it gets real quiet, I'll say, 'Don't mess with me! I could open a vein and take out the entire front row!' "

Moore copes with his illness, and life, with humor. "In my group therapy," he says, "there's a woman with breast cancer who just had a mastectomy. Everyone in the group goes for that victim thing: 'Are you OK? Can I get you anything?' I'm like: 'Hey, Nancy . . . Nice tit!'"

"She laughed.

"My T-cells went up.

"It was a lovely afternoon."

HIV can stand for many things. When Moore told his parents, who live in Virginia, about his illness, Moore says they thought *HIV* stood for *Homosexuals in Virginia.* In the medical world, *HIV* stands for *human immuno-*

deficiency virus. For a troupe of Los Angeles comedians, it stands for *Humor Is Vital.* One member of this group, whose husband died from AIDS, wants people to know that "it is important to communicate the message that AIDS touches everyone in the population."

The group does this by poking fun at the disease and showing others that they can do the same:

"I know what you are thinking. Oh God, not another blind Orthodox Jewish gay with AIDS comic."

"I've got herpes, I've got AIDS, I guess you can say I'm an incurable romantic."

"AIDS. Finally, a diet that works!"

Danny Williams, the gay comedian mentioned in an earlier chapter, also helps his community cope through comedy. Williams jokes about a man he knew who had KS (Kaposi's sarcoma) lesions all over his body. The man gave himself the nickname Dot. "He would wear polka dot shirts and anything he could find that had lots of dots."

Others, like the late filmmaker Peter Adair, helped form a support group for people who are HIV-positive. As part of his belief that humor is a way of tolerating the intolerable, Adair named the group the Virus Club. Its slogan is "I'm dying to get in."

To outsiders, this kind of dark humor may seem inappropriate or offensive. However, coming from someone dealing with this illness, it is not only appropriate but also (and perhaps more important) life affirming.

AIDS has been a cosmic kick in the ass—a challenge to finally begin living fully.

—MICHAEL CALLEN, *Surviving AIDS*

HELLO, HIV

Marty Carls is a remarkable man who is living with HIV, the precursor of AIDS. I have known Marty for many years—years before *AIDS* was a household word, years before he was HIV-positive.

Marty is a different person today than he was years ago. Yes, he had a sense of humor then (and still does). Yes, he lived life fully then (and still does). But he didn't seem to possess as much respect for life then as he does now. *Exercise, diet,* and *medication,* for example, were words not found in

Marty's vocabulary. I remember walking down the street with him as he consumed a pint of ice cream. Then, because he hadn't had enough, he headed for the grocery store for another, and then seriously considered whether he should purchase a third.

Author Edmund White once wrote, "The prospect of ill health and death inspires a new sense of urgency." For Marty, this could not be more true. Being HIV-positive has helped him see his life in a new light. It has sped up his personal growth. He readily acknowledges that this illness has been the best thing that ever happened to him.

Others might think of HIV as the beginning of the end, but Marty has reframed it. For him, it is the beginning of a new life. "Being HIV-positive," he says, "has taught me to be very much in the here and now. I now live so much more in the moment because I realize *that* is the most significant thing. HIV has been a catalyst for me to love myself more, for me to value my connections with friends and with my relatives. It has been an opportunity for me rather than an enemy.

"Every single day when I wake up, I greet my HIV. I greet it with joy. I thank it for supporting me in feeling so much better about myself and the things in my life. When I go to sleep each night, I thank my HIV for being part of my life."

The lesson learned here is often ignored by those of us who are not ill. But it is an important one for all of us to cultivate. Perhaps one newspaper columnist said it best: "AIDS and its deathly specter force us to pay sharper attention to the art of living."

In keeping with his positive attitude, Marty wants an AIDS quilt panel memorializing him made *before* he dies. That way, he says, he can enjoy it while he is still around. With ironic humor, Marty declares that with the new AIDS medications, which are keeping patients alive longer, he will likely die from something other than AIDS and will never get a panel with his name on it after all. "Such a problem," he says, "we should all have."

....

Finding out that you or someone you love is HIV-positive, or has AIDS, is never good news. It starts a chain reaction and your life will never be the same. But, believe it or not, amazing good can come along as a result of this heartbreak. It can be a wake-up call to live life. As strange as it may seem, for a surprising number of people learning they are HIV-positive leads to a more optimistic and productive life than ever before.

—MARK DE SOLLA PRICE, *Living Positively in a World with HIV/AIDS*

....

Happier Than I've Ever Been

Not being HIV-positive or having AIDS myself, I find it hard to comprehend how anyone with this kind of illness can find anything good about it. Yet I frequently hear people with this and other life-challenging illnesses say, as Marty did, that it is the best thing that ever happened to them. Here, for example, from *Voices That Care,* are two women's views of their disease:

> What do I see when I look in the mirror? Probably the most vibrant and alive and happy person that I've ever seen. For the first time in my life I'm not looking at whether or not my hair is in place or my lipstick is on straight. I am looking at my soul, and I'm pleased with what I see.

> HIV has allowed me to be more vocal. It has allowed me to look at myself and know that I can make a difference. I'm not as shy as I used to be in most situations. I think I'm more outgoing. You know what? I'm happier than I've ever been.

Author Michael Callen, in his book *Surviving AIDS,* wrote similarly about the AIDS and HIV-positive people that he interviewed. "What stood out from the interviews," said Callen, "was an ineffable quality of *joie de vivre*—a friskiness. These people didn't just believe that life was worth living—they all said in their own way that life was worth *celebrating,* and they were each busy doing precisely that. I can't say whether feeling incredibly grateful and glad to be alive is the cause, or the result, of having survived; probably both."

One person with AIDS, like the women above, observed that "in a strange way . . . even though my circumstances are worse, I feel happier because of what I've learned and what I've seen. There's a kind of confidence that comes only with the truth; even when things are horrible all around you, you still feel empowered because you know your own truth. I'm talking about the truth that's inside of you."

Callen, who had AIDS himself, felt much the same way as some of the people he interviewed. "While I would never have wished for AIDS," he says, "the plain truth is that I'm happier now than I've ever been. . . . AIDS has taught me the preciousness of life and the healing power of love. . . . I've tried to see AIDS as a challenge to begin living, instead of a sign to begin dying. . . . AIDS forced me to take responsibility for my own life—for the choices I had made and the choices I could still make. For better or worse, AIDS has made me the man I am today."

And that man, even though he is no longer alive, had a sense of humor. One of the things he jokingly attributed his longtime survival to was Classic Coke. He said, "Whenever I'm feeling low and looking for a reason to keep struggling, I remind myself that sugar is a sufficient reason to live."

The only way to get through whatever olympics we're engaged in is by firing up a sense of humor and pressing on.

—JAMES KIRKWOOD, *P. S. Your Cat Is Dead!*

THE HUMOR TOOLBOX

Brian Craft and his wife, Kelly, call themselves "option counselors." I met them via the Internet, where I discovered a listing of the seminars they offer. One of the programs, entitled "Humor and Other Grave Subjects," uses comedy, in part, to deal with grief and loss. I called them up to interview them and found that they not only teach people how to find laughter in loss; they live it.

In addition to being a hemophiliac and having gotten HIV through a blood transfusion, Brian has had a subdural hematoma (a bleeding under the lining surrounding the brain); he has had his spleen removed and his gall bladder taken out. Being a former stand-up comedian, Craft jokes, "Basically, if I don't get five minutes of funny material out of anything major that goes wrong with me, what's the point?"

Craft says finding humor in illness is a behavior choice. Growing up as a hemophiliac was a challenge. Craft said his family always had him look for the upside of his condition. "All of us, at one time or another, have been dealt hands that we don't like, whether it's terminal or temporary. If you decide to look for the humor in your situation, and you make it a choice, then the humor will start showing up." He asks, "Did you ever decide to buy a car? Suddenly you see that car everywhere."

Craft also asks, "What are the options? To me, being sad and in pain is worse than being happy and being in pain. Even if it's just briefly, humor reminds us, especially when we are grieving, that there is more to life than just the pain."

Craft jokes that there is even absurd humor in his medications. "My doctor gave me pills to help me sleep. On the container is a big red sticker that says, 'Caution: May Cause Drowsiness.'

"Also, in the morning, I take ten pills. One of the bottles says: 'Take on an empty stomach.' The other one says: 'Take after a full meal.' So," says Craft, "I count the first pill as a full meal and then take the other pill." When I asked Craft if he had anything else he wanted to add before we concluded our interview, he said, "I think people need to realize that humor is a tool like any other tool which we use to access and to cope with things. If we don't add humor to our toolbox, we are missing a great versatile device to deal with the blows that life can throw at us."

One afternoon after leaving his room, we all gathered in the hospital lobby and burst into uncontrollable laughter. Eddie was just not a suitably noble dying person. We loved him, but he was, in fact, a huge pain. Our laughter was the only possible release, the only way we could return to Eddie's bedside for further abuse. At that moment, I knew that for everyone, AIDS would require a truly exquisite and deranged sense of humor.

—PAUL RUDNICK, author of *Jeffrey*

LAUGHING MATTER

While many AIDS patients suffer the anguish of dealing with such things as dementia, experimental drugs, low T cells, and KS lesions, others find these to be grist for the humor mill. Things that cause problems in the first place suddenly become laughing matter. As one person jokingly put it, "Laughin' somehow manages to get the blood flowing back in your poor, tired, anemic veins . . . so you can get yourself over to the drugstore for more drugs!"

By using fantasy, exaggeration, play, and an attitude of joy, people with AIDS, or those who are HIV-positive, have been able to get a brief humorous break from their distress. Here follow some of their humorous observations about this disease.

• *On the loss of memory*
  In my day, we used to refer to this [dementia] as "havin' an attack of the vapours." It was a very useful technique we all picked up at Miss Yardley-Smythe's Finishing School for Belles. I suppose this dementia thing gives it an air of medical respectability, but it seems to me that being Southern, a Belle, and genteel is all the justification one needs for throwing ashtrays, crystal or tantrums.

My friend, I'll call him Frank, had been taking care of another friend, Dan, who moved back to Atlanta from Los Angeles. Unfortunately, Dan developed dementia shortly after he arrived and ended up hospitalized. He was a former Marine officer and spent most of his time as a Drill Instructor.

One morning, Dan announced that his last company of trainees were coming to visit him in the hospital. He was very upset because none of them knew the "Marine Corps Hymn." He began to insist that Frank, who is a music teacher, teach his company the hymn right there in the hospital room. Dan was pleased that Frank would take on this chore but concerned that because of the large number of trainees, they would not be able to see him. So he insisted that Frank stand on the bed to practice directing the company.

About this time, the nurse walked in with the morning medications to find Frank on the bed with both him and Dan singing at the top of their lungs. It took a meeting of the doctor, the Director of Nursing and several of Dan's friends to talk the hospital into letting Frank come back again.

• *On taking drugs*
Several years ago, I along with about eight other guys started an informal support group. Most of us at that time were new to HIV and didn't find a lot funny about it; that quickly changed. During our first meeting, several of us had those lovely little pill timers and they all went off at the same time. Being the proper hostess, I grabbed a candy dish, dumped a whole bottle of AZT and passed it around. One of my friends looked at the guy next to him and said, "You know you're in a nice place when they serve AZT."

• *On low T cells*
While I was walking down the hall, I almost collided with my startled roommate as he was coming out of his room. He said to me, "Well, you just killed 10 T-Cells!"

Our favorite amusement is waiting until your count gets low enough so that you can name them all. Let's see—Tommy T-Cell, Terry T-Cell, Trixie T-Cell. . . .

• *On KS lesions*

One of my good friends, Gary, had decided to go into the clothing design business. He is designing a line called "Lesion Wear" by Gary (of course). Unlike Barbie's peel-and-stick lesions, you can wear some of these and not pull out what remaining hair is left on your legs. This will be a complete line from sleepwear to Lesion Suits.

....

I found that when I was laughing, I wasn't depressed! I wasn't scared! I managed to forget my anxieties for awhile! I always felt relief from the incredible stress of trying to sort out my life with AIDS and cancer. And no matter how many blood tests or biopsies or bureaucrats I had to deal with, I always had that laughter to look forward to at the end of the day. It really kept me going.

—THE REVEREND A. STEPHEN PIETERS

....

FANTASY

Throughout my investigation of humor in the dying process, I have been intrigued by how some people, whether caregiver, bereaved, or patient, can find humor in their situation while others can't. I've asked a number of people who were able to do it how they managed it. Most don't know—most people, that is, except Mark Feldman.

Feldman battled AIDS in the very early days of the disease. It was a time when doctors knew little about it and even less about how to relieve its symptoms. In spite of this, Feldman used humor to deal with his pain and anguish. When I interviewed him, he showed me a gold spray-painted king's crown. He told me that he wore it from time to time to remind him that he still had some power over his illness.

Feldman used fantasy and his playful imagination to detract from the long, tedious, and often painful medical procedures. While lying on the examining table, for example, he would entertain himself by fantasizing himself on the ceiling looking down at an elaborate medical game.

What Feldman was doing was something that kids often do but adults frequently forget. He was playing in his imagination. Kids know that in their mind they can always transport themselves from somewhere they don't like to somewhere they do. "When you are in the hospital or very sick at home and are very lonely," advise terminally ill kids in *There Is a Rainbow Be-*

hind Every Dark Cloud, "just sort of day dream about something pleasant . . . by using our imagination, we could do anything."

In addition to playing in his imagination, Feldman joked around with the medical staff. He says, "It helps the process for me. It also helps the doctors and nurses. These procedures are not easy for them either." Feldman told so many jokes, in fact, that when he had his bronchoscopy and could not talk, one doctor kidded, "Well at least now Henny Youngman will be quiet."

Another time, when medical personnel wanted to see Feldman's KS lesions in his mouth, he would request an admission charge before he would open his mouth and allow the curtain to go up on "his" show. He also proposed that the title of his memoirs about his illness be titled *Kaposi Dearest.* Once he mockingly offered himself to be the KS poster boy. "Keep your sense of humor," advises Feldman. "Let me tell you, it helps a lot."

When I asked Feldman, who was the first person I interviewed about humor and AIDS, how come he was able to find humor in spite of what he was going through, he gave me the most succinct, most telling, and perhaps the best answer to my query I have heard thus far.

He said, "You know, it's more fun that way."

EXAGGERATION

A common technique comedians use to get a laugh is exaggeration. Take any situation, exaggerate it until it becomes absurd, and you too will probably see some humor in it. The example below, found on an HIV/AIDS chat line, shows how one person effectively used this technique.

> A gay local newspaper writer pointed out to me the other day that, in our little community, the gays have overrun the supermarket and are becoming more obnoxious than the housewives or retirees could ever hope to be. When other people go shopping, they gossip about PTA information and compare the latest baseball scores.
>
> When us "hometown" gays go to the supermarket and meet in the aisles or the parking lot, we gossip about symptoms/meds information and compare the latest CD4 scores.
>
> Antigens and antipasto. Chicken and liver function. Melons

and melanomas. Bactrim and NutriSlim. Videx and Windex. TB and TV Guide. Tetracycline and Mr. Clean. Shingles and Pringles.

Someone suggested switching to another supermarket, where you can pick up your meds and groceries in one stop (you can get your IV bags and Baggies at the same time that you get your pictures developed). I can just see someone at the checkout counter: "Meow Mix—$1.45, AZT—$145, cranberry juice—$1.37, Videx—$137. Total due—$461.78. Have a nice day!"

An acquaintance of mine, Duncan Campbell, used exaggeration to find a bit of humor in the medications he was taking—medications that were supposed to cure but often made things worse. In his poetic book *Candle in the Night: Fours Seasons in the Life of a Man with AIDS,* Campbell amusingly writes:

> We got to joking about the possible drug side effects they don't warn you about, and how refreshing it would be to see a list that went something like this: diarrhea, bone-marrow depletion, mental changes, bleeding, bruising, nausea, stomach upset, pale skin, fever, headache, blurred vision, ringing in ears, sore throat, dizziness, tingling of the hands and feet, increased appetite, loss of appetite, nervousness (so who wouldn't be, by this point?), mental changes, financial ruin, divorce, suicide, IRS audit, forgetting to water the garden, not understanding why the cat won't eat dinner on the same plate she just cleaned up after your partner fed her five minutes ago, death, extreme creativity, joy, dread, you name it—we got it.

PLAY

One man told me that he found out that he had AIDS on April 1. Although his diagnosis was no April Fool's joke, he continued to find humor in what he calls, as if it were a national TV show, "the Wonderful World of AIDS."

For most people, doctor's waiting rooms and examining rooms are no laughing matter. Not for this young man. Coming from a creative, art and theater background, he played with these tense medical surroundings and frequently found something to laugh about.

On waiting in doctors' examining rooms, he says with a chuckle: "If the doctor keeps me waiting, I go through all the drawers in the exam room. I unwind the bandages and redecorate the room with them. I hang them from the blinds. I swag them from the light fixtures. I wrap them around the table legs. When the doctor comes in and wants to know what I've done, I say, 'I'm homosexual. I'm redecorating. I might as well make myself at home!' "

A friend of mine lost his lover to AIDS. Shortly after, he got a renewal notice for a magazine to which his lover subscribed. On the outside in big red letters it read, "You're About to Expire." My friend sent it back with his own message on the front: "You're Too Late!"

—BEVERLY PATTERSON-HAMILTON

ATTITUDE OF JOY

"I don't consider myself to be funny," the Reverend Dr. A. Stephen Pieters said, "but I'm sure humor had something to do with my cancer going into remission and my recovery from AIDS."

These are remarkable statements, considering that the Reverend Pieters not only is a long-term survivor of AIDS but has had, among other illnesses, pneumonia, herpes, shingles, hepatitis, a variety of fungal infections, candidiasis, valley fever, mononucleosis, Kaposi's sarcoma, and lymphoma.

Knowing that his prognosis was not very good, Pieters pursued every avenue of healing he could. That's when he encountered Norman Cousins's book *Anatomy of an Illness.* Pieters made it a point to begin and end each day by watching a TV sitcom. He also asked his friends to send him jokes instead of letters and get-well cards because "I discovered that when I was laughing, I couldn't be depressed. I couldn't be anxious. I couldn't be scared. It was like taking a vacation in the midst of all of the chaos."

Several years ago, Pieters was selected to become the first patient to test the first antiviral drug, Suramin. Within three weeks all his KS lesions had disappeared. A short time later both the KS and lymphoma were in remission. Although it was wonderful news for him, the drug proved to be ineffective for other AIDS patients. In fact, almost one quarter of the people who were on the drug trial died.

"So, what was the added extra ingredient [that healed me]?" Pieters asks. "Some people will say it was God. Some people will say it was meditation and visualization. Some people will say it was laughter. Some people will say it was a combination of all of the above. I don't really know. All I know is that I've always been aware of the importance of laughter."

About visiting others with AIDS, Pieters remarks, "Whenever I go into a room of someone who is dying of AIDS, I go in with an 'attitude of joy.' And that attitude of joy is what sets the scene for laughter."

In keeping with his attitude of joy, Pieters parodied the song "I Am the Very Model of a Modern Major General," from Gilbert and Sullivan's operetta *Pirates of Penzance*. He turned it into "I Am the Very Model of a Medical Anomaly," with his own witty and inventive lyrics about his miraculous medical recovery:

> *I am the very model of a medical anomaly.*
> *I've had KS, lymphoma, hepatitis, thrush, and CMV,*
> *Bacterial pneumonia and adrenal insufficiency;*
> *All this and more because I caught a virus they call HIV.*

> *But then I took an antiviral, just like chemotherapy.*
> *It made me sick, my hair fell out, I suffered neurologically.*
> *But hey! It worked: it stopped all of the HIV activity,*
> *Lymphoma's in remission, and there is no more KS to see!*

> *Chorus:*
> *Lymphoma's in remission, and there is no more KS to see!*
> *Lymphoma's in remission, and there is no more KS to see!*
> *Lymphoma's in remission, and there is no more KS KS to see!*

> *And now a decade later, I'm as healthy as a horse can be.*
> *It surely is a miracle for anyone with faith to see.*
> *But still in journals medical, and scientific inquiry,*
> *I am the very model of a medical anomaly.*

> *Chorus:*
> *But still in journals medical, and scientific inquiry,*
> *I am the very model of a medical anomaly!*

I asked Pieters about his advice to others with AIDS. He said, "Well, I think it is important to find something to laugh about every single day because every single day there is certainly something not to laugh about."

In April of 1984, Pieters was told he had eight months to live. I interviewed him at the end of 1996. At the time, he was the director of AIDS ministry at the Universal Fellowship of Metropolitan Community Churches. He is still doing that, still going strong—and still laughing.

Can't Afford Not To

First off, I can never, ever feel exactly what someone with AIDS is going through. But I do believe in laughter. There's an old saying: "Laugh in the face of death." Well, I think it needs to be revised to "Laugh in the face of life." Laughter inspires longevity.

—JAY THOMAS

The gay community, which has suffered the biggest blow from the AIDS epidemic in the U.S., has found ways to lighten up their plight. In doing so, they have shown other patients who are battling other diseases that it need not all be solemn.

Readers not associated with someone who is going through such a devastating illness as AIDS may ask, "How can anyone in that condition possibly laugh?" Perhaps the question should be, "How can they afford not to?"

For the answer, I turned to my friend fellow humorologist and clinical psychologist Steve Wilson, who once wrote that "humor and laughter get us through situations that might otherwise seem completely unbearable."

"Laughter," said Wilson, "doesn't take the tragedy and disappointment out of life, but for a moment gives us another way of looking at it. And in that moment we may be distracted enough from our predicaments, or see them just differently enough to recover some physical strength or gain some peace of mind."

Wilson provides us with a wonderful example of this from the movie *Philadelphia,* in which Tom Hanks plays a lawyer who is dying of AIDS. The lawyer is on his deathbed. He is saying his final good-byes. He is weak and tired as the last of his strength is waning. And he musters up a joke.

Commenting on the movie, Wilson says, "At the moment of death, about to cross the threshold of our greatest accelerated learning and enlightenment—the dying person proffers humor, and (when another character repeats it in the next scene) it is passed on like the Olympic torch, a flame that ignites hope and gives us a glimpse of the possibility that life is not futile and can, although the days of this life are limited, be extraordinarily worthwhile. Humor does that."

That is exactly what many courageous people with AIDS, or other life–challenging illnesses, either consciously or unconsciously know. That is why they use humor. That is why they can't afford not to.

Chapter 9

Kids: Great Wisdom from Small Fry

So never let a cloudy day ruin your sunshine, for even if you can't see it, the sunshine is still there, inside of you, ready to shine when you will let it.

— AMY PITZELE, nine and a half years old, in
We Are Not Alone: Learning to Live with Chronic Illness

You've Got to Be "Kidding"

When Erma Bombeck was doing research for her book about children with cancer, she felt that as an adult she brought along too much pity and emotional baggage. But the kids cured her of that right away. "One asked me," she says, " 'would you be happier if we cried all the time?' So I figured, why not laugh with them?"

Kids have a way of dealing with illness in a much lighter way than adults. Because of this, they can be an encouraging resource for terminally ill patients who are looking for ways to lighten up their own predicament. Because their experience has not yet been corrupted by the world around them, children can be wonderful teachers. They have much to offer adults.

For example, in their playful minds, kids instantly transport themselves to other places—something that can be useful to seriously ill adults in pain. Kids are also spontaneous and "tell it like it is"—adults, on the other hand, frequently try to avoid the reality of someone dying. And because of their innocence, children's unencumbered views of a serious situation often produce comic, and sometimes insightful, comments.

Kids are also very wise. The severely ill children who contributed to *There Is a Rainbow Behind Every Dark Cloud* have some sage advice for adults. They say, "You can learn to control your mind and decide to be happy 'inside' with a smiling heart in spite of what happens to you on the 'outside.'"

The children who authored that quote are part of the Center for Attitudinal Healing, in Sausalito, California. Its founder, Gerald Jampolsky, M.D., knows the importance of humor. In a magazine article written about his work, Jampolsky describes an encounter he had with a young hospital patient. It illustrates a lesson most of us need to master—to stop being so serious.

> Her name is Angela and I met her in a Baptist hospital in Jacksonville. She was only six, and she had leukemia. Her hair had fallen out at one time and she had had liver biopsies, bone biopsies—you name it. But it was as if none of that stuff had ever happened. She was one of the happiest kids in the world, giving her love and light away. I had just met with the hospital administrator, who was dealing with a major conflict between the medical and surgical departments. I said to Angela, "See that guy? He's sad right now because some people are upset with him. But I know that's not as big a problem as facing a life-threatening illness. Can you say something that might help him?" The moment I said that she put her hand to her face and I thought, I shouldn't have asked that, it's such a big question for such a little kid. And all of a sudden she took her hand away. She smiled and she said, "Oh, mister, I know what you could do. Go out and buy a feather and tickle him three times a day." I sent this administrator a feather and told him the story. And on days when I'm overly serious, I use my imagination and tickle myself with a feather and think of Angela.

The child-related stories in this chapter can teach us a lot about turning tears to laughter. When, for example, one youngster was asked if there was anything positive about death, he replied, "Yes. You don't have to tie your shoelaces anymore."

Turning Tears to Laughter

If you can't handle optimism, don't go around children with cancer. . . . If they have one leg, they will jump into a puddle of water with it. If they pass a mirror reflecting their bald head, they will stick out their tongue in defiance. If you put 'em in a wheelchair, they'll find another one to race.

—ERMA BOMBECK

THE CHEERIEST PLACE IN THE WORLD

For those who can see only the dark side in the death of a child, Viktor Frankl reminds us that we cannot judge a biography by its length—"Sometimes the 'unfinished' are among the most beautiful symphonies."

One man I interviewed, named Forrest, agrees with Frankl. He had a twelve-year-old daughter who died of cancer. In a letter to a friend, he spoke about the lighter side of his daughter's death and the strength she gave him through her courage:

> You know, this month it will be sixteen months since we began to deal with all the horrors of leukemia, and yet, although the sadness and grief is with us all, as I think of it now, I also have memories of countless funny, touching, profound and beautiful moments. . . .
>
> One would think that it would be a sad experience—life on a pediatric ward—but it was not. In fact, it is the cheeriest place in the world, because as children always do, they create fun for themselves; their business is to deal with their pain first, and then to get on with their real business, which is to find joy. . . .
>
> Of course, it is sad that children have to be sick and that some die, but one of my favorite philosophers once said that "the length of things is irrelevant; only in height is there joy."

Forrest told of how his daughter talked about her "little oxygen tent on the prairie" and how they played balloon ball in the hospital—"Can you imagine her chasing a silly balloon carting along an I.V. pole?"

If you want to work with dying children, it would be useful to be able to eat their tears.

—STEPHEN LEVINE, *Who Dies?*

CLOWNING AROUND

In *How Can I Help?* by Ram Dass and Paul Gorman, the authors write about a clown who visits hospitalized children. The pain and suffering the clown sees is almost too much to bear until one child shows the clown how to do it:

> There was this one little black kid. . . . He was horribly burned. He looked like burnt toast. . . . It was just terrible, just mind-boggling. My jaw dropped, I gasped, and I came completely unglued. I remember flashing back to the antiwar movement. There was a picture of a napalmed kid I used to carry around at demonstrations. Suddenly here was that kid right in front of me. Unbelievably painful to behold. . . .
>
> So there we were, burnt toast and unglued clown. Quite a sight. . . .
>
> All of a sudden, this other little kid comes whizzing by—I think he was skating along with his IV pole—and he stops, and kinda pushes around me, and looks into the crib at this other kid, and comes out with, "Hey. YOU UGLY!" Just like that. And the burnt kid made this gurgling laugh kind of noise and his face moved around, and all of a sudden I just went for his eyes, and we locked up right there, and everything else just dissolved. It was like going through a tunnel right to his heart. And all the burnt flesh disappeared, and I saw him from another place. We settled right in. "YOU UGLY!" Right. He ugly. He probably knows how ugly he is more than anyone else. And if he's gotta deal with people hanging around with saliva coming out of their mouths, it's gonna be extra horrible. But if somebody just meets him in the eye and says, "Hey, what's happening? Wanna hear a riddle . . . ?"

Although authors Dass and Gorman do not state who the clown is, I am pretty sure that they are writing about Wavy Gravy. Among his other achievements, Gravy is the man who ran a pig for president in 1968; a board member of the Seva Foundation, which raises millions of dollars each year to help prevent blindness in third world countries; and someone who has the distinction of having a Ben & Jerry's ice cream named after him.

In his own book, *Something Good for a Change,* Gravy relates one of his other encounters with a child in the hospital:

> That's me now, putting clown-white makeup on little Billy. I often use makeup as a connection to children of all ages. I let them watch me put on my makeup and it helps to demystify the sometimes scary clown vibe. Billy was about eleven and needed no demystification. This kid was ready for anything. And so was his little sister, who said, "We could show the movie on Billy's head."
>
> I looked down at my handiwork and sure enough, I had covered Billy's entire head with clown white. The chemo had long since claimed his hair so Billy was bald as a billiard ball, and his little sister was right! We could indeed show the movie on Billy's head. (We had *Godzilla* cued up to project on the wall of the day room instead.)
>
> "Could we, Wavy Gravy? Could we please show *Godzilla* on my head?"
>
> There was no way I could deny such a bizarre and heartfelt request.
>
> "Okay Billy, you got it! But promise to tell me if your neck gets sore and we'll shoot the movie back up on the wall." I figured the kid wouldn't make it through the credits.
>
> So there we all were, sitting around eating popcorn and watching *Godzilla* on Billy's head. Billy is positively glowing with delight and I must confess my mind had already entered the train wreck zone—just when I thought things couldn't possibly get any weirder . . . in walked a team of visiting Japanese doctors here to inspect the unit!

....

God made most people with perfectly shaped heads. The rest he gave hair.

—ANONYMOUS

....

BALD IS BEAUTIFUL

At the age of six, Jason Gaes was stricken with a rare form of cancer, Burkitt's lymphoma. After two years of treatment, he was free of cancer. He was determined to tell other kids that they too can survive this disease, so he turned his illness into a gift. Without adult help he wrote *My Book for Kids with Cansur.* Among other things, he talks about being bald. (*Note:* the spellings are his.)

> Sometimes keymotharupy makes you sick and you throw up. Sometimes you looz your hair from it but you can war hats if it bothers you. Mostly kids don't care when your bald. And if they laff or make fun there not very good friends anyway. Some kids think its cool.

Gaes also finds something positive about being bald, having cancer, and surviving it. He writes:

> When your bald you don't have to worry about getting shampoo in your eyes. When your sick from a treatment you get to stay home from school and when your done having cansur you get to have a big party. The best party in your whole life.

And finally, he has sage advice for both young and adult patients:

> The rest of the days when you don't have a treetment try to forget you have cansur and think about something else. Shoot baskets or go swimming.

Dr. Bernie Siegel often quotes Gaes in his cancer workshops. He says that "in one page Jason tells what it takes me an entire book to say, because he is a native. He has also been one of my teachers—though I spell better than he does."

THE CHEMO CUT

Like the adults in the chapter on cancer, kids too have found that they can joke about being bald. In *I Want to Grow Hair, I Want to Grow Up, I Want to Go to Boise,* for example, Erma Bombeck shares the humor that surfaced as a result of kids' not having hair. The following three brief excerpts come from a chapter entitled "The Chemo Cut":

> When three-year old Carrie's blond curls were all gone and little fuzz was starting to grow back, she observed with curiosity her father's balding head as he bent over to tie her shoe. "Daddy," she asked, "is your hair coming or going?"

> David was entering his sophomore year at school and figured he'd let this T-shirt do the talking. The front of it read, "So what are you staring at . . . some of my teachers are bald too." When he turned around, the second part of the message read, "Only I'm better looking."

> One evening as she [Samantha] readied for bed, she begged her mother to sleep with her. Her mother used her seventeen reasons not to, ending with the one that has always worked with kids: "Gee, Mommy and Daddy have to share a bed, but you're so lucky you get a bed all to yourself." Samantha wasn't buying. She still wanted to sleep with her mother. Finally, her mother turned to her daughter, exasperated, and said, "Samantha, give me one good reason why I should sleep with you."
>
> With large brown eyes she looked up and said, "Because I don't have enough hair to twist and you do!"

Kids frequently use their imaginations to deal with and lighten up their pain. A colleague of mine, Charles Moyer, told me about how his eleven-year-old son handled the huge scar that resulted from a baseball-size tumor being removed from his chest.

Whenever Moyer's son took his shirt off, other kids would ask, "What happened to you?" He would look them straight in the eye and with a serious expression on his face reply, "I got bit by a shark."

Bombeck, in another part of her book, also talks about the creative ways kids handle their illness-related adversities. Here, for example, are a few of their responses to why they have no hair:

"The wind just blew it out."

"My father is Kojak."

"I just joined the Marines."

Bombeck suggests that adults who have the Chemo Cut might take a lesson from kids and come up with creative answers to the question "What happened to your hair?" Bombeck says her own might include:

"I sold it."

"I traded it for this body."

"I was having a makeover and ran out of money."

....

When Karen was turning five, she was very conscious of her birthday and becoming very aware of the world around her, of which she was definitely the center. Who was this guy Lincoln who was getting all the attention on her birthday? She wanted to know all about him, and since she couldn't see him, I tried to explain about death. Not long afterward, our family dog, Smokey, was hit by a car and died at the vet's. When I broke the news to the children, it was their first experience of death. Karen's response was, "Now there's two guys dead—Lincoln and Smokey."

—ELLIE MAREK, PHOENIX, ARIZONA

....

DIRECTING DONAHUE

In their book *Lighten Up,* C. W. Metcalf and Roma Felible describe an incident on the Phil Donahue show where a young boy, in a child's outspoken manner, tells it like it is:

Phil zeroed in on a boy about ten years old. The child had a Spanish surname, dark hair that fell across his forehead, almost covering his eyes, and an ivory-toothed grin.

Phil paced off with his elbow-flapping impression of a gull about to take flight. "Here you are, so young, with cancer, I mean, a disease that—you know—might lead to your, well, gee, *to your death,* in a very short while. But you seem happy. I don't get it!" Flap-flap. "It seems so . . . *unfair."* . . .

The boy cocked his head slightly to one side. "Well, gee," he began with that wry grin—was he mimicking Phil?—"my life is more than having cancer, you know. At the Center [for Attitudinal Healing], we help each other, and I guess that keeps us from feeling too sorry for ourselves."

Phil held the microphone close to his lips. "But if I were in your situation I'd be, well, I don't know, but I think I'd be *really* scared! How can you be so brave?"

The child cracked a smile. "Calm down, will ya. I don't know why *you're* so upset. *I'm* the one who's sick."

....

When my daughter was little, we drove past a cemetery and she asked what it was. I told her that's where they keep people after they die. She then asked, "What are they keeping them for?"

—CECILIA MACDONALD, NORTHERN CALIFORNIA

....

STARS AND STRIPES FOREVER

Betty L. Boyce, a California writer and consultant, told me the following amusing story about her fourteen-year-old granddaughter:

It was the first time for just the two of us after my husband's sudden death. My son brought her with him after getting that shocking phone call and they joined the other family members who were able to come home.

This time alone together was a gift to us—and we talked about many things, including her grandpa's death. I shared one of the events she had not been privy to at the time. The funeral director had ingratiatingly apologized to me for "having to use so much makeup to cover the facial injuries—especially the one above the eye."

My husband had died so quickly that morning out jogging that he did not have time to protect his face when he fell. He had a broken nose and various abrasions—the one above the left eye was the most severe. Without a heartbeat of hesitation, I said, "You should have checked with me. I would have told you to use a Band-Aid!" Obviously my remark was unexpected—the funeral director was aghast, and speechless. "Of course!" my granddaughter responded at the end of the story as rapidly as I had to the funeral director. "A Band-Aid certainly would have been better than all that goop—a Stars and Stripes Band-Aid!"

I have a card hanging in my shower with diagrams showing how to perform a breast exam. Usually I leave the card with the pictures facing the wall. One day, however, the cleaning lady left it turned outward. My 7-year-old-son, Jake, saw it and asked me what it was for. Without going into much detail, I told him it was there to remind me to do something every month and to show me how to do it. Jake replied, "Mama, I can't believe you don't know how to wash your boobs."

—J ANE H ILL writing about Peggy Johnson, in
Chicken Soup for the Surviving Soul

SHOW AND TELL

Christine Clifford overheard the following conversation between her young son Brooks and one of his friends, named Rishi, as they were playing in a tent in the backyard:

Rishi: What's the matter with your mom again?
Brooks: Well, she's got cancer.
Rishi: Is she going to die?
Brooks: No, I don't think so.
Rishi: Well, her head looks like a baseball. Do you think she'd let us autograph it?

Clifford, who is in remission from cancer, agrees that children can help us laugh when we are ill. She suggests that if you don't have children in your life, you should find some: "Your own children, nieces, nephews or if you don't have a resource, volunteer somewhere to be around children. They are such a source of inspiration."

"First and foremost," states Clifford, "children do not understand the seriousness of your situation." It is because of this innocence that some of the outrageous things they do or say are funny. For example, Clifford says, "I was home from the hospital for about three days, and flowers were coming in by the droves. My son answered the doorbell and found a delivery man standing there with another box of flowers. My son yelled up to me, 'Mom, more flowers for your breast!' "

Clifford knows that when anyone in a family gets cancer it affects everyone in the family. Therefore her second book, *Our Family Has Cancer, Too,* consists of cartoons just for children. It's obvious that her two sons,

Brooks and Tim, provide her with lots of material. In addition to her kids' comic comments, Clifford told me about a bittersweet moment that occurred with one of her son's friends.

The day after I got home from the hospital, my son asked me if he could have a friend over. I said he could. When the bell rang, I answered the door, and my son's little friend (I say "little" because he was the smallest child in the second grade) said to me, "Mrs. Clifford, I hear you have cancer."

He said it so loud that it reverberated though the house— "CANCER!"

"Yes, David, I do," I answered.

"Did they get it all?" he asked.

"Well, we certainly hope they did, and what they didn't get we are going to get in some treatments over the next six months."

"Well, Mrs. Clifford, I just want you to know that I said a prayer for you, and I hope you feel better."

With tears in my eyes, I stooped down face to face and said, "Thank you so much for saying that. It really made me feel good."

"No problem," David replied as he was coming in the house.

"By the way, David, how did you know I had cancer?"

Before David could answer, my son, who was inching his way down the staircase, shot me one of those looks that only a kid can give you and said, "Mom, I shared it with my class during Show & Tell!"

....

Two young kids were talking at a funeral. One asked the other, "What happened to your grandfather? Did he break something and die?" The other girl responded, "No. He just got sick and died." Consoling her friend, one child said to the other, "Well that's okay. My grandfather got sick and they had to put him in a box like that too."

....

ONE TEAR AT A TIME

In providing lighter moments in serious times, a child's innocent words not only tickle our funny bone but sometimes warm our heart as well.

"My son was only ten months old when his father died in a motorcycle accident," said Susan Corpany, author of *Unfinished Business*. "Scott being so young was oblivious to the grief I was going through but because he was just a happy, cheerful little baby it helped me cope a lot."

"One day," says Corpany,

Scott ran out of the house stark naked and, thinking I could not see him, hid behind an open-meshed chain link fence. Suddenly I thought: "What if I was the one who died and I looked down and saw my husband just going through life, the way I am— going through the motions but not with much joy? And what if I had left this beautiful playful little boy and I saw my partner not enjoying him?"

Then it hit me. It was the humor of seeing my naked son crouched behind that fence—it drained all of the anger out of me. At that moment, I resolved that I was going to find things to enjoy in life. It was a turning point for me to realize that no matter what we have lost or gone through we can still find joy. It took my little boy to show that to me.

I told Corpany that when my wife died, the person who gave me the most comfort was my daughter, Sarah. Even though she was only ten, even though she didn't quite know what was going on, she somehow understood.

After Ellen died, Sarah and I would go for a walk or get an ice cream, and we would talk about Mommy. And we would cry, and we would laugh. Sarah was always the one who was there for me without a lot of "stuff" getting in the way.

Without realizing it, kids frequently do kid stuff that jolts us out of our grief. Corpany shared that several months after her husband died, she was alone on her wedding anniversary. "There wasn't much to celebrate after your partner is gone but I had decided that I would get flowers and take them to the cemetery," she says.

I got the same type of floral arrangement that we had at our wedding. I put the flowers and Scott, who was about a year-and-a-half at the time, in the back seat of the car. When I got to the cemetery, I reached in the back to get the flowers. During our drive, Scott had pulled all the flowers off the stems. Of course, I couldn't yell at a cute little boy who kept repeating "Fowers,

Fowers." So I took the dead flowers and stems over to the grave, threw them down and yelled, "Happy Anniversary."

It took me a little while to see the humor in the situation, but when I told the story to a friend we both started to laugh.

Corpany notes, "There are some aspects of grief that you never laugh about or see humor in. But it is not so much a matter of laughing at what happened as it is laughing at some of the events or the circumstances it puts you in."

Another story Corpany shared struck me because, in part, it illustrated how laughter and a small child can help us cope with grief.

Years ago I sat in the kitchen of my newfound friend, Rondi, another young widow I had been put in touch with through mutual friends. Our friendship was a blessing to both of us, to find someone who understood the hazards of losing a partner at an early age, with young children to care for. Her phone rang. It was her father. After talking to him for a few minutes, she said, "My friend, Susan, is here. You know, the one who lost her husband, too." It struck me, the funny ways we use to describe death, and I piped up from the background, "Yes, he wandered down the wrong aisle in the supermarket and I haven't seen him since." It struck her funny, and soon her father was holding on the phone, listening to the two of us laughing. After she calmed down and continued the conversation, a confused man on the line said, "Well, I'm glad that you both find this situation funny. . . ."

Perhaps what worked for us was that we were experiencing the same loss, and it was safe to laugh about it together, because neither of us was trying to diminish the painful reality of our situations. I cried with her when she received the autopsy report that said that her husband was burned on ninety-eight percent of his body. She commiserated with me when I got a bill for storage of a totaled vehicle that I didn't even know was in storage, and did not want to see and certainly did not want to go "claim." . . . Laughter can lift a person's spirits, and it need not have anything to do with their present situation. A humorous movie can help someone to escape for a couple of hours. Children (too) can be a blessing. When I would cry, my little son would toddle to the bathroom and come back with little postage-stamp pieces of toilet paper, one at a time, to dry my tears. Soon I would be laughing, because of his sweet efforts to dry my tears—one tear at a time.

In one of our correspondences, Corpany wrote a follow-up to the story above. She noted that Scott, the "little" boy with the pieces of toilet paper, is now fifteen years old, over six feet tall, and growing facial hair. She said that the anniversary of her husband's death fell on Father's Day this year. "I knew that someone at church would give a talk or there would be a song that would get the waterworks started, so I was prepared. Both my pockets were stuffed with tissues. When Scott noticed me starting to get weepy, and as I reached for a tissue from my pocket, he took it away from me. 'Wait a minute,' he said. He then tore off a small corner and handed it to me, knowing it would make me smile."

I HAVE EVERYTHING

Discussing her own bout with cancer in the October 1992 issue of Redbook magazine, Erma Bombeck revealed how one youngster's wise remarks about cancer gave the humorist a new perspective about her own disease.

"Last year," Bombeck wrote, "an estimated 165,000 women survived breast cancer. Every time I forget to feel grateful to be one of them, I hear the voice of an eight-year-old named Christina diagnosed with cancer of the nervous system. When asked what she wanted for her birthday, she thought long and hard and finally said, "I don't know. I have two sticker books and a Cabbage Patch doll. I have everything!"

Chapter 10

Lingering Loss

I never would have made it if I could not have laughed. It lifted me momentarily out of this horrible situation, just enough to make it livable.

—VIKTOR FRANKL, concentration camp survivor

The people in the preceding chapters faced death due to a life-threatening illness. The people in this chapter faced death because the fullness of their living was threatened by either a severe disability or prison walls. Nevertheless, many of these people dealt with their lingering loss through humor.

Humor and Loss of Self

Laughter sets the spirit free to move through even the most tragic circumstances.

—CAPT. GERALD COFFEE, prisoner of war

There are a number of chronic diseases, such as Alzheimer's and multiple sclerosis, that rob their hosts of the person they once were. For many people, dealing with such illnesses is like dealing with the living dead. They find nothing funny about it. Others, however, as the following stories illustrate, have managed to find something to laugh about in spite of the severity of the disease. Before I share their stories, however, first a caveat.

There is a big distinction between the funny things that caregivers and families find in dealing with patients and the insensitive, inappropriate humor exhibited by others. As in humor revolving around other illnesses or loss, it's okay for those who are close to the pain to joke about it; those who aren't, shouldn't.

In that light, here are some examples of the comic relief that has helped caregivers cope.

THE POSITIVE, SOMETIMES HUMOROUS, SIDE OF ALZHEIMER'S

"Over the past five years," says Edward Ahern of J2S2 Online Productions,

I've been caregiver to my aunt, who has Alzheimer's disease. During those years I've heard people talking about how horrible this disease is. However, I don't see it. I see this disease as something that's far less horrible than some of the other diseases of the aged. Throughout these five years, my aunt has given me more and more reasons to believe this philosophy:

• What disease allows an eighty-seven-year-old woman to once again be an eight-year-old girl—and enjoy it?
• Each and every day my aunt goes through her pocketbook, she finds new and exciting things in there—even though they were there when she checked five minutes ago.
• While once upon a time she needed diamonds and furs to make her happy, now it takes nothing more than a McDonald's Happy Meal toy to make her day.
• She had two teeth pulled the other day. As I was present while this was done, I saw how they yanked and pulled until the teeth were free. This would have been painful even to the strongest of men. However, when we got to the car after the appointment, my aunt had no recollection of what had happened. She only wondered why there was cotton in her mouth.
• Each day, she attends specialized Alzheimer's day care. However, she thinks it's school and that she's needed there each day. This gives her a sense of being needed—a great thing.
• When at a loss for what to do to occupy my aunt's time, I give her a basket of laundry to fold. When she's done, I take it in the other room

and unfold it and throw it back in the basket and bring her more. This can go on all day.

• My aunt has not a problem in the world. The most catastrophic thing for her is not having some type of jewelry on. No violence, death, sickness, world havoc, or crisis can stir this graceful old woman. She can watch a thirty-minute special report on some demented subject like child murder or rape, and her only comment after the news story is something like, "That's a nice tie he's wearing."

• Stress? What is that? Most Alzheimer's patients won't know. Not because they don't remember the word, but because, for the most part, they have none. Ain't life wonderful?

Ahern has come to this conclusion: "So while I know Alzheimer's can be a debilitating disease that can rob people of their personalities, I can also see how some aspects of this disease aren't nearly as bad as we think. After all, every cloud has a . . . now what color was that lining?"

....

What is a benefit of having Alzheimer's?
     You get to make new friends every day!

....

While Alzheimer's itself is not funny, funny things do happen because of the nature of the disease. For example:

• One woman said her husband, who had advanced Alzheimer's, hid the grandchildren's Easter eggs and then had equally as much fun finding them!

• Another woman found a romantic side to her husband's illness. "He forgets who he is married to. He proposes to me every morning."

• Still another woman, who has a mother-in-law with Alzheimer's, told her young children, "You'll never run out of anything to say. Everything is a brand-new story."

• And finally, a friend of mine has a mother with Alzheimer's. When it came time to discuss her burial wishes, he asked whether she wanted to be cremated or buried. His mother replied, "Surprise me!"

For Linda Combs, a woman from North Carolina, dealing with her mother's Alzheimer's has definitely been a long good-bye. Combs's mother has had the disease since she was fifty-one. For twenty-two years, Combs has seen her mother slowly lose her sense of self.

Combs described how her mother would always bring her roll-on deodorant to the dinner table and set it down next to her plate. When asked why the deodorant, Combs's mother would not respond. It was as if she didn't even know it was there.

One time, during yet another deodorant-on-the-table meal, Combs's husband, without a hint of a smile, asked, "Would someone please pass the deodorant?"

....

Don't Forget the Alzheimer's Meeting on Thursday Night

—SIGN IN A HOSPITAL

....

The nature of humor in Alzheimer's, as of the humor found in other areas of loss, is bittersweet. On the one hand we find something laughable, but on the other hand we would rather that disease were not the source.

I found the following bittersweet humorous story on-line:

Shortly after we brought my mom home to live with us, we went out shopping to a mall. I left my wife, Donna, and my mom together for a few minutes. Later that evening after mom had gone to bed, Donna told me what happened after I left.

Mom waited while Donna looked at some clothes. Pretty soon my mom started talking to this lady she saw standing by her. Donna said that mom was nodding her head and making pleasant comments. Donna stood and watched for a few minutes. Then Donna felt like they should go, so she took mom's arm and started to move. Mom turned to her and said that the other lady was really nice but that she was sure hard of hearing.

Mom had been talking to herself in the mirror.

We had a good laugh but at the same time it was tragic that mom was unable to recognize herself in that mirror.

Computer on-line services provide a wonderful way for people to share information about a disease that they or their loved ones are facing. Through their humorous anecdotes they also validate how humor helps them cope. Here are two stories that were posted on an Alzheimer's bulletin board:

I'm reminded of a story about my grandmother who probably had Alzheimer's but at the time was called "senile." She was in her

90's and had raised eleven children. One time when I was visiting, one of her daughters stopped by. We all had a nice long chat and Grandma was very loving and sweet with my aunt. After my aunt left, Grandma turned to me and said, "Who was that fat lady?"

The other day I got a phone call at the office from my Mom. She was really angry at herself and said she couldn't find her hearing aid. Then she asked, "But you can still hear me, can't you?"

Those not taking care of a person with Alzheimer's may not see the humor in some of this. They find Alzheimer's humor startling. They may think that it is cruel to laugh in such circumstances. The truth is, there are so many eccentric manifestations of Alzheimer's that if the caregiver doesn't laugh about some of them, their tension may explode in other, more harmful ways.

One caregiver who is taking care of two Alzheimer's patients offers this advice: "If I laugh, we have a good day—we enjoy each other's company. If I cry, we have a horrible day. I don't think they want to be around me. Alzheimer's patients mirror our emotions, which is why our sense of humor is so important."

Still, as therapeutic as humor might be in these situations, some people feel uncomfortable laughing at some of the bizarre things Alzheimer's patients do or say. One respondent, for example, said, "I felt guilty sometimes when I've thought that something Mom did was funny. I have quietly laughed about things, but I always felt really badly that I did. However, just hearing others share their humorous items on the Alzheimer's bulletin board has helped me accept that there are many facets to this mess."

Nothing, no experience good or bad, no belief, no cause, is in itself momentous enough to monopolize the whole of life to the exclusion of laughter.
—ALFRED NORTH WHITEHEAD

YOU ADJUST TO WHAT SHOCKS YOU

"If I tell someone I made a film about my mother and it's about her having Alzheimer's, they get an extremely long face and say, 'I'm so sorry.'

And then I tell them, 'No, actually I've made a humorous story about my mother who has Alzheimer's.' Then, if anything, they would think that I'm just this insensitive weird person."

So states Deborah Hoffmann, director of the Oscar-nominated documentary *Complaints of a Dutiful Daughter.*

How could anyone make a funny film about a disease that is so devastating—a disease that cruelly erases past memories and replaces them with confusion? Hoffmann has an answer for her critics: "Without being disrespectful to my mother and her situation, I admitted this is a funny situation. In any other setting everybody would laugh. . . . And once I let myself ease up and see the humor, my mom felt a lot better. She enjoyed laughing about all this."

"Little by little," Hoffmann says, "you adjust to what shocks you."

In her film, Hoffmann describes several periods her mother went through. First came the Dentist Period, when her mother was obsessed with a dental appointment and showed up daily at the dentist's office even after her teeth were fixed. Then came the Hearing Aid Period, with piles of notes and phone messages concerning the status of a broken hearing aid. Then the Lorna Doone Period, with boxes of cookies showing up everywhere. And with equal absurdity there were also, among others, the Ticket Period, the Suitcase Period, and the Banana Period.

Funny, or frightening? On the surface, horrifying—until Hoffmann frees herself from the burden of caring by stepping back, seeing the situation for what it is, and eventually finding joy in it.

Hoffmann discovers her liberating moment when she realizes that she can respond to her mother at her mother's level rather than trying to correct her. For example, what did it matter if it was May and her mother thought it was April? Or what did it matter if her mother thought that they had both been in elementary school together?

Hoffmann has an important message for others who are taking care of someone with Alzheimer's. She learned that laughter can be liberating. When we get caught up in the moment-to-moment detail of a situation, we lose perspective. When we step back and see the bigger picture, we might even see some humor in it.

"Once you accept the parameters," says Hoffmann, that "my mother has Alzheimer's and it's true she is going to be remembering less and less and less, and she may very rarely know who I am—if you can accept that—it can still be a very joyful life."

I was talking to a group of people who had multiple sclerosis with associated bladder problems and I mentioned to them that they had a great gift or benefit. Whenever you walk into nursing homes or hospitals you always see triangular signs reading "Wet Floor." I asked them, "How many times have you ever done it?" I haven't changed their bladder or their neurological condition, but I have changed their view of the world so that they no longer see their affliction as terrible, and they can begin to laugh at it once in a while.

—BERNIE SIEGEL, M.D.

BUT YOU JUST CHECKED IN

Eleven years ago, when I first thought about becoming a professional speaker, I heard a woman give a presentation that blew me away. She used a combination of the spoken word and music to get the audience to both laugh and cry. When people asked me what I wanted to be when I grew up (as a professional speaker, that is), I said, "I want to be Rosita Perez."

Rosita is still wowing her audiences, and I am still learning from her. But these days she does it with a little more effort, due to her having multiple sclerosis. Yet, Rosita and her wonderful husband, Ray, have not let this debilitating disease deplete their sense of humor.

When I asked Rosita how she manages to find anything to laugh about in her illness, she says Ray is her lighter side. He is not only her wheelchair pusher but her humor pusher as well. "I have a very dark side that needs lightening up," Rosita reveals, "and his timing," as revealed in the following story, "is impeccable." She says:

> One of the realities of MS is an overwhelming fatigue that can render me tired very quickly. Knowing that, one day Ray picked me up at the airport after I was coming home from a speaking engagement. While we were waiting at the baggage carousel, he handed me a key. It was obviously a hotel key. I said, "Why? Did I forget to turn this in? Did I just drop it?"
>
> He said nothing but "Follow me."
>
> We proceeded to where the car was parked and he put my luggage in it. Instead of getting in the car and driving off, however, he said, "Follow me."
>
> Up the escalator we went. Suddenly we were in the lobby

of the Marriott airport hotel. I kept saying, "What? We live half an hour from here. Why a hotel? I just got home!"

"Follow me," was all he said.

As he opened the hotel door, he explained that sometimes, by the time we get home, I am tired, and he wanted to make sure I still had some energy for him because he had missed me A LOT.

Two hours later, as he was checking out of the hotel, the very young woman behind the desk looked up in astonishment. She said, "But, Mr. Perez, you just checked in. Was everything all right?"

"Everything was TERRIFIC!" he said with a huge smile.

Humor and Loss of Independence

With humor not only do I feel more whole inside, and not only do I feel closer to those about me, but I also feel a quality of elevation, raising the realm of consciousness to a space that is larger than before . . . humor has more than comforted me through some difficult times. It has helped me make sense and meaning of my disability.

—ARNOLD BEISSER, M.D., POLIO SURVIVOR

There are many levels of disability. There are also many ways to handle being incapacitated. The following stories are from people who have used humor, in part, to compensate for the loss of independence. You will notice that I have made little comment about these stories. Most of them speak for themselves.

FUNNY AS A CRUTCH

Dr. Arnold Beisser is a former national tennis champion and a polio survivor. In his uplifting book *Flying Without Wings,* he gives us some understanding of humor's role in disability:

There is an expression, "funny as a crutch," which is used to suggest that there are some things that are so tragic that there is no room for humor. To say that there is nothing funny about a crutch may seem obvious; however, I can assure you that for those people who use crutches there is much they find that is funny about them. Wherever disabled people congregate, whether on a hospital ward or in an independent living group, or simply when friends gather together, there is an "in" humor that deals exactly with the frustrations and predicaments of being disabled. Though these things may seem tragic or shocking at the time, and certainly would appear so to the nondisabled, they may have a very different effect on those who have spent their lives with disability. They have learned that, like any other aspect of life, there is an underside of wheelchairs, braces, crutches, and other appliances which can be seen as humorous.

A group of my friends, who were patients at the rehabilitation hospital when I was there, get together frequently. We are all still disabled. There are many things we found humorous then, and still laugh about now on occasion. The day that Lyle became so angry at a fellow patient that he tried to take a swing at him, even though he was unable to rise from his bed. The day that Andy became trapped in midair, in a patient transport device, and the attendant could not get him down. Then there was the time when a paralyzed patient was floating in the swimming pool supported by an inner tube which gradually lost its air. The look of utter despair on his face as he slowly began to sink below the surface now creates gales of laughter when it is recalled (of course, he was rescued). There are scores of such instances which in their own context we experience as hilarious.

NOW MY CALVES DON'T CRAMP

In his extraordinary book *The Theft of the Spirit,* author Carl Hammerschlag writes about a physically challenged man with a bold sense of humor:

As an eighteen-year-old, Hugh was already considered one of the best competitive rock climbers in the country. Caught in a blinding blizzard while on a climbing expedition, he strayed from his intended route and crossed a snow-covered stream, breaking through the ice into the water below. His feet were soaked and rapidly freezing; blinded by snow and exhausted, he built a rudimentary shelter. After two days, rescuers found him under a sprucebough lean-to, nearly dead from hypothermia and severe frostbite. Both his legs had to be amputated just below the knees.

Five weeks after the amputations, with new artificial legs, Hugh climbed a steep trail near his home. Within a year, he'd learned to design and make himself new feet. For walking, he screwed in a fairly flexible, natural-shaped foot. He created feet for specific climbing conditions. For most climbing, he used a stiffer, narrower foot. To climb a rock wall with narrow crevices, he switched to a stiff foot with a rubber nub on the end that he could jam into the cracks. For ice climbing, he used a foot fitted with a neoprene bootee and crampons.

In competitive rock climbing, the various routes up a cliff are rated from 5.0 to 5.13 according to difficulty. Few climbers are able to do anything above 5.10. Hugh is doing 5.10 ascents, sometimes without ropes.

When asked by a reporter what it was like to climb now, as compared to the old days, he said, "Now my calves don't cramp."

SHAKY SPEAKER

You can tell from the name of his company that Nicholas Peterson, a man who has been living with Parkinson's disease for twenty-one years, has a sense of humor about his disability. The name of his business? Shaky Speaker Presentations.

To open his program, Peterson takes his handicap sticker, puts in on the back of the chair, which is center stage, and says, "This is the only way they will let me sit here without being towed."

Right off the bat he lets his audience know that his condition is something that he can laugh about. "My humor," he says, "is directed at myself but it's done with affection. That's the key to it. If it's loving humor then it is healing and it is a bonding experience.

"One of the things that happens with Parkinson's disease," says Peterson, "is 'freezing spells'—muscles get stuck and I can't move." Peterson recalls being in the art supplies section of a department store. "I was standing there, more and more tense, and more and more embarrassed about it, when

I looked up and realized—there I was, *stationary* in the *stationery* department."

People like Peterson can poke fun at their disability because it is part of who they are. Others, however, who don't have a disability should not. Peterson provided an example related to this from a movie called *Waterdance*. It's about three men who are in a rehabilitation hospital for their spinal injuries. One night, tired of hanging around the rehab facility, they steal the hospital van for a joyride. When they just miss getting into an accident, one of the guys remarks to the other disabled two, "Thank God. We're already paralyzed!"

People say, "Alex, why no sunglasses?"

I say, "Hey, I don't see deaf people wearing earmuffs."

—ALEX VALDEZ, blind stand-up comedian

BALLET LESSONS

As previously noted, sometimes a little bit of laughter can be a great icebreaker and a way of getting communication going. In their book *No Time for Nonsense,* authors Ronna Fay Jevne, Ph.D., and Alexander Levitan, M.D., write about Grace, "a very obese older woman who was referred for severe pain in the stump remaining after her right leg was amputated":

> She had many grievances directed against the doctors who had previously cared for her, as well as anger resulting from the situation in which she found herself. One day she was sitting in her wheelchair with her amputated stump visible, feeling somewhat self-conscious about being noticed by other patients, when one of the office staff returned from lunch and noticed her sitting there.
>
> "How are you doing, Grace?" she asked.
>
> "Fine," Grace replied in a soft voice.
>
> "And how are the ballet lessons coming?"
>
> At this point Grace began laughing so hard that she nearly fell out of her wheelchair. All the other patients were laughing too and were waiting for her reply. It didn't take long for Grace to come out with, "Wait 'til you see my tutu!"

WELCOME TO HOLLAND

Emily Perl Kingsley is a talented writer of children's books and the mother of a child with Down's syndrome. In the following story, which Kingsley authored, she reminds us that we can be happy wherever we are, even if that place involves dealing with a lifelong disability.

I am often asked to describe the experience of raising a child with a disability—to try to help people who have not shared that unique experience to understand it, to imagine how it would feel. It's like . . .

When you're going to have a baby, it's like planning a fabulous vacation trip—to Italy. You buy a bunch of guide books and make your wonderful plans. The Coliseum. The Michelangelo *David*. The gondolas in Venice. You may learn some handy phrases in Italian. It's all very exciting.

After months of eager anticipation, the day finally arrives. You pack your bags, and off you go. Several hours later, the plane lands. The stewardess comes in and says, "Welcome to Holland."

"Holland?!?" you say. "What do you mean Holland?? I signed up for Italy! I'm supposed to be in Italy. All my life I've dreamed of going to Italy."

But there's been a change in flight plan. They've landed in Holland and there you must stay.

The important thing is that they haven't taken you to a horrible, disgusting, filthy place, full of pestilence, famine and disease. It's just a different place.

So you must go out and buy new guide books. And you must learn a whole new language. And you will meet a whole new group of people you would never have met.

It's just a different place. It's slower-paced than Italy, less flashy than Italy. But after you've been there for a while and you catch your breath, you look around . . . and you begin to notice that Holland has windmills . . . and Holland has tulips. Holland even has Rembrandts.

But everyone you know is busy coming and going from Italy . . . and they're all bragging about what a wonderful time they had there. And for the rest of your life, you will say, "Yes, that's where I was supposed to go. That's what I planned."

And the pain of that will never, ever, ever, ever go away, because the loss of that dream is a very, very significant loss.

But, if you spend your life mourning that fact that you didn't get to Italy, you may never be free to enjoy the very special, the very lovely things . . . about Holland.

Humor and Loss of Freedom

Can laughter be restorative in a case as extreme as the Holocaust? That something so slight should alleviate the burden of something so gigantic might, on the face of it, be a joke itself. But then, humor counts most in precisely those situations where more decisive remedies fail.

—BEREL LANG, *Writing and the Holocaust*

Humor has incredible power. It can both belittle us—if we are too close to the subject being mocked—or help us rise above that which belittles us.

Humor's dual personality became very clear to me one day when I was giving a talk to a group of Jewish women. Near the beginning of the program, something I said caused a participant to ask about "Jewish princess" jokes. When she did, the audience went wild.

"How could you possibly discuss such an offensive subject in front of this group?" they wanted to know. (Mind you, I was not the one who mentioned it; nonetheless, I was being blamed.)

Then things got worse. One person said she wasn't exactly sure what a Jewish princess joke was. So, to my horror, someone else in the audience provided an example:

"What does a Jewish princess make for dinner?"

"Reservations."

Now the audience was really furious. I knew I could no longer go on with my prepared program, so I set aside my notes and, after the audience calmed down, discussed humor's dual power. I talked about how it can both oppress us, as did the Jewish princess joke that just offended them, and liberate us. To illustrate the latter, I turned the discussion to the awesome power humor had to help those in concentration camps withstand the atrocities of the Holocaust.

Replete with death and the smell of burning flesh, a concentration camp is the last place one would expect to find humor. Yet in his book *Laughter in Hell: The Use of Humor During the Holocaust,* author Steve Lipman says that "scores of books in German and the other languages of the liberated countries . . . document aspects of humor's omnipresence."

"Nothing about the Holocaust was funny," notes Lipman, but humor was "the currency of hope"—and other than prayer, probably the only hope there was. Humor was, according to this author, "both a psychological weapon and a defense mechanism. It was a social bond among trusted friends. It was a diversion, a shield, a morale booster, an equalizer, a drop of truth in a world founded on lies. In short, a cryptic redefining of the victims' world."

We are discussing concentration camp victims here. But the same redefining of one's world with humor holds true of anyone involved in a life-challenging circumstance, whether it be a death camp or a disease, an internment or an illness.

Perhaps the best-known example of the use of humor in the death camps is that of psychiatrist Viktor Frankl. At Auschwitz he found even the smallest joke gave prisoners a sense of hope, something to look forward to each day, power over their oppressors, and detachment from their horrific surroundings.

With a fellow comrade, Frankl would invent at least "one amusing story" a day. He tells, for example, of the time a prisoner turned to one of the capos (favored prisoners who acted as guards) and said, "Imagine! I knew him when he was only the president of a bank!"

In addition, in order to have something to look forward to, Frankl would joke with another prisoner about life after liberation. In his book *Man's Search for Meaning,* Frankl describes how inmates might invent "amusing dreams about the future, such as forecasting that during a future dinner engagement they might forget themselves when the soup was served and beg the hostess to ladle it 'from the bottom.' "This was because in the camps the meager pieces of solid food sank to the bottom.

If nothing else, humor gave the death camp prisoners a diversion. But in that diversion it also gave them a device to oppress their oppressor. One inmate, who was a youngster at the time, recalls:

> We mimicked top overseers and I did impersonations about camp life and somebody did a little tapdance, different funny, crazy things. The overseers slipped into the barracks while we weren't looking, and instead of giving us a punishment they were laughing their heads off. I couldn't believe it: one day they were hitting us black and blue, and then they were laughing while we made fun of them. But, you see, in spite of all our agony and pain

we never lost our ability to laugh at ourselves and our miserable situation. We had to make jokes to survive and save ourselves from deep depression.

After researching thousands of examples of humor during the Holocaust, Lipman concludes, "I am more sure than ever that humor is one of the greatest gifts God gave mankind to pull itself out of despair."

Still, you might ask, "How could victims of the Holocaust laugh in the face of death?" The answer is, "How could they not?" For like prayer, humor was an inner strength that could not, as everything else had, be taken away from them.

> The very act of making fun of our inferior position raises us above it.
> —HARVEY MINDESS, *Laughter and Liberation*

Now Plant the Potatoes

During the early stages of the Nazis' anti-Jewish persecution, a squad of Gestapo agents raided a farm on the outskirts of Berlin. The husband, a Jew, was taken to a concentration camp. His wife, a gentile, remained behind. She was able to smuggle a few letters in and out of the camp.

In one letter she complained that she was unable to plow the field and plant her supply of seed potatoes. Her husband considered the problem for a few days, then openly mailed a letter in which he ordered her to forget about plowing the field. "Don't touch a single spot," he wrote. "That's where I buried the rifles and grenades."

A few days later, several truckloads of Gestapo agents again raided the farm. For a week they dug in the field, searching each shovel full of earth for a trace of the guns and grenades. Finally, finding nothing, they left. Confused, the wife wrote her husband another letter, describing the raid. "The field," she related, "has been sifted from one end to the other."

The husband wrote back: "Now plant the potatoes."

Humor: The Currency of Hope

Hasidic Tales of the Holocaust is not a happy book. It is a collection of sometimes grim, sometimes hopeful anecdotes from those who survived the atrocities of the concentration camps. Although there are a few stories in this book that have a hint of humor, for the most part miracles play a bigger role than mirth.

So why am I including a story from that book in this one? Because it contains one tale that provides a lesson both about hope and, in some parallel way, about humor.

Among the newly arrived victims was Elaine Seidenfeld from Chust. . . .

On her first night in Auschwitz, on the top of a three-tiered bunk, squeezed like a sardine among twelve other young women, she was initiated into the hell of Auschwitz. . . . "Today it is them, tomorrow it will be us," said one emaciated girl from Poland. . . .

"Not I," protested the horrified Elaine, "I will survive: I want to live and find my husband."

"You are new here," replied the girl from Poland. "Once upon a time we all wanted to live, but it is useless."

"I want to live," Elaine was pleading with the girl. "I must live, I must find my husband." No one responded to her plea. In the distance someone was screaming and then it was silent again. Only Elaine was still whispering, "I want to live, I want to live."

[Four months later] Elaine was marched out from *Lager C* with about 3,000 other women inmates. They were marched in the direction of the gas chambers. The closer they got to the gas chambers, the more feverishly Elaine repeated the only plea she had uttered since she came to Auschwitz: "I want to live, I want to find my husband." They reached the gas chambers. The march halted. . . .

[Later] they were loaded on sealed cattle cars, about 150 girls to a wagon. . . .

"I want to live," she kept repeating. "I want to live. If only I could find some promising sign, something I could believe in, something, just anything, something that will indicate that I will live."

The train jolted, the boards near Elaine were groaning, a slit of light appeared. Between two boards a crack was formed. Through the tiny crack she saw the clear blue sky . . . and there in the bright blue skies was a straight pure-white line. Joy overcame Elaine. She felt that her prayer was answered, that heaven had given her a sign that she would indeed survive and live. . . .

The train arrived at Stutthof. Soon the girls were to learn that Stutthof was no improvement over Auschwitz. Many died from hard labor, hunger, and lack of water; others were taken to the gas chambers. But not Elaine; she was lucky. . . .

As the Russian front was nearing Stutthof in January 1945, Elaine and 26,000 other women were evacuated. Many were drowned in the Baltic Sea, others were sent on the long death march. Thousands fell along the road. . . . But Elaine marched on. Dressed in a single summer dress with a pair of shabby clogs, she held on to her white line of life. . . .

Then it was over. The war ended, the guns were silenced. . . .

Lone survivors . . . were going home to search for remnants from a vanished past. They passed through the same train stations, traveled on the same tracks that just months before led to the gas chambers and fed the chimneys. Now they were heading "home." Elaine was on her way to Chust. Then, on a crowded train platform, she saw her husband board a train to Chust also.

Thirty years later Elaine was asked, "What do you suppose that white line you saw really was?"

Elaine answered, "You see, in order to survive you must believe in something, you need a source of inspiration, of courage, something bigger than yourself, something to overcome reality. The line was my source of inspiration, my sign from heaven."

For Elaine it was a sign in the sky. For others, like Viktor Frankl, it was humor—humor that provided, as did the white line in the sky, something to believe in, a source of inspiration to keep going, and something to replace reality.

HUMOR: THE TOOL OF SURVIVAL

Concentration camp prisoners were not the only ones to use humor to endure. Research of survival literature has shown that humor is among the most frequently mentioned coping mechanisms.

"This held true," says Jim Mitchell, Ph.D. (onetime chief of psychology services for the U.S. Air Force Survival School at Fairchild Air Force Base), "for survivors sampled from a broad range of extreme situations that left people stranded or on their own for extended periods, such as survivors of POW camps, natural disasters, expedition mishaps, and plane crashes in remote areas."

As pointed out earlier, humor may not be evident, or even appropriate, in the heart of a crisis, but, notes Mitchell, "it seems to play an important role in facilitating long term survival after the initial crisis has passed."

Mitchell's words are important when compared to studies showing the health risks for those who have lost a loved one. Just as for POWs, concentration camp prisoners, and other survivors of disasters, humor can be an important factor in the management of their stress, their emotions, and their survival.

Natan (Anatoly) Sharansky knows about humor and survival. He was in Soviet prisons for nine years, which included sixteen months of solitary confinement and the death sentence.

To invoke fear in Sharansky, the Soviet secret police—the KGB—would taunt him with the word *rastrel,* which means "firing squad." "The first thing I get accustomed to is that they can kill me." To counteract the fear, he says, "I protected myself with humor. I started talking often of the firing squad, making jokes about it. You make jokes fifteen or twenty times and the word becomes like any other word. The ear gets accustomed to it and it no longer prompts fear."

Again, as we have seen elsewhere, humor became a powerful tool in a powerless situation.

Comedian Yakov Smirnoff, who also grew up in the Soviet Union, used this tool too to fight repression. Although his situation was not life threatening like Sharansky's, the curtailment of his freedom was oppressive. So after getting out of the country and coming to America, he poked fun at Soviet repression.

The first time he went into a restaurant in this country, he says, they asked him how many were in his party. He answered, "Two million."

Smirnoff also jokes about an uncle who wrote to him about a new TV show in the Soviet Union. It's about a couple living in Siberia. It's entitled *Thirty Something Below Zero.*

Instead of allowing their government's attitudes and persecution to diminish them, both Sharansky and Smirnoff added humor and triumphantly turned tyranny around.

The things that strike us as funny have the power to set us free.
—R O N J E N K I N S, *Subversive Laughter*

HUMOR: THE CONVEYOR
OF FREEDOM

One final note about humor and freedom. Laughter can break those chains that limit our freedom—not always physically, of course, but they can mentally release us from that which confines.

In *Subversive Laughter: The Liberating Power of Comedy,* Prof. Ron Jenkins writes about the power of humor to liberate. For example, he was in Johannesburg, South Africa, where he stopped to watch a demonstration. Suddenly he was caught up in the protest and mistakenly carted off to jail with the demonstrators. He writes:

> In defiance of their captors, the protesters began joking and singing protest songs as soon as the caged door of the prison van slammed shut. When we arrived at the jail, the music and laughter flowed out of the vans into the cells. It brought a feeling of familiarity to the bleak gray jailhouse. Everyone knew the words to the protest songs from having sung them for years. The more people the police stuffed in, the more festive the mood became. Before long there were over six hundred men in the cell and spirits were skyrocketing. When an exhausted prisoner suggested we take a break from singing and dancing, one of the revelers laughed, "Why should we be quiet? We can do anything we want. We're in jail!"
>
> The man had shouted, "We're in jail" as if it were a cry of emancipation. Here in the cell these blacks were determined to escape the invisible prison of apartheid and act as free men. Having been arrested at gunpoint and caged in a cell so cramped it was almost impossible to sit down, the men laughed at the injustice of their situation until it couldn't hurt them anymore. Surrounded by hostile police, they formed a collective organism that responded to threats with protective roars of laughter.

Laughing at our oppressors gives us a double whammy. We have, paradoxically, both taken control of the situation and also given up trying to control it. When we poke fun at our plight, we are accepting it without forcibly trying to change what is happening, and at the same time we are overpowering our opponent. As the humor in the concentration camps showed, prisoners who used it were better able to accept their grim surroundings and at the same time feel that they had a verbal advantage over the guards.

Laughter also gave prisoners hope because laughter is like prayer. In both, we go beyond the world as we know it. Both transcend our predicament. We may not like the situation that we are in, but laughter helps us rise above it.

"Perhaps it is more than coincidence," writes Jenkins in the preface to his book, "that people who laugh in the face of death are often the ones who live to tell about it. . . . Laughter is not our only defense against despair, but it can play a key role in freeing us from the stresses that sap our will to live."

Chapter 11

Sudden Loss

When we understand the part that humor plays in the range of coping mechanisms people use to confront experiences of loss, even so-called gallows humor takes on a certain respectability.

—LYNNE ANN DESPELDER AND
ALBERT LEE STRICKLAND, *The Path Ahead*

This chapter will explore humor and its relationship to the threat of sudden death, death that can come as a result of an accident, suicide, or disaster.

I do not know which is worse—sudden death or a lingering loss. Neither is pleasant. Each, like everything else in life, has its advantages and disadvantages. In an interview I did with a woman whose son died instantly in a shooting accident, we discussed both. "On the one hand," she said, "you get a chance to say good-bye. On the other hand, watching your loved one suffer is very difficult. Then again, having what you think is a normal day and then the sheriff drives up and tells you that your son has been shot and killed is horrendous."

We came to no conclusion. Perhaps there isn't any.

Humor and Fatal Accidents

If you can find humor in anything, you can survive it.

—BILL COSBY

Perhaps it is easier to find instances of humor in lingering death, where a family or loved one has time to adapt to the loss, than in the shock of a sudden death. However, as the following story shows, the healing power of humor can be found even here.

The narrative was sent to me by a woman named Sandy. Her husband was killed in a commercial airline crash. It took her a while to find any humor in her life again after her husband's death, but when she did, it made a major difference.

> The time frame was about a month and a half after the crash. USAir had erected a huge memorial including all the names of the victims and had chosen Sewickley (our home town) Cemetery as the site for the memorial. Survivors (strange how they called us that—I called myself a victim) of the deceased were invited to participate in a dedication ceremony at the memorial. The ceremony, of course, was highly publicized in the press, as was every little detail about the crash and the people involved. I had been hounded by the press—even out-of-state reporters called to ask if I would talk to them—"up close and personal." So I knew that this ceremony would be a media circus even though we were assured that security would be tight.
>
> I obviously wanted nothing to do with it. So my friend Cheryl suggested that we drive to a new mall that had just opened, about an hour away from here, where no one would recognize me and I could avoid the whole scene. As we were walking around the mall (I was still in that foggy state of mind where you are just going through the motions of living but not really knowing why), the funniest thought hit me from out of nowhere. I began to laugh out loud and told Cheryl why—I had had a vision in my mind of Chuck and his dad watching over me. Chuck was saying, "They are dedicating a memorial to me today, and what is she doing? SHOPPING! SANDY'S SHOPPING! TYPICAL!" We both had a good laugh and I felt a short period of relief, because now I knew that it might be possible to laugh and to feel alive again, even if it was in small doses.

After I read Sandy's story, I called her to find out if humor had played any other role in her recovery. At first she didn't think so. Then she talked about how her work for the past year had been to get her kids back in order and to bring the family together again. "I found that humor really helped here," she said.

"The kids had a lot of anger—they resisted getting up in the morning for school; they would be sitting at the breakfast table scowling at me and poking at each other. So I would do to them what they did to me. If they were sitting there with a big frown on their face, I would mimic their face to show them what they looked like.

"One of the things I was trying to correct was the way they were answering me. All their responses to my questions were in a smart-alecky way. I would ask a simple ordinary question—like, 'Do you want strawberries in your cereal today?'—and they would fire back an answer in a very curt and harsh manner. So I would ask them to answer me again, but this time in a polite but very exaggerated tone of voice. Like, 'Yes, dear mother, we would like some strawberries today.' "

What Sandy found was that the kids would laugh as they learned that their anger wasn't directed at such things as the strawberries. The technique worked so well that soon it became embellished and elicited even bigger laughs. "Yes, dear mother, sweetest mother, most beautiful mother, best cook, thinnest mother in the world, we would love some strawberries today."

Humor and Suicide

Razors pain you;
Rivers are damp;
Acids stain you;
And drugs cause cramp.
Guns aren't lawful;
Nooses give;
Gas smells awful;
You might as well live.
—DOROTHY PARKER

Perhaps the worst kind of sudden loss is suicide. In other life-challenging situations, people want to survive, and some turn to humor as their ally. Suicide, on the other hand, is about people who don't want to survive. Humor tends to be almost nonexistent.

According to Robert Litman, M.D., who researched hundreds of suicide notes, "Suicidal people seem to have lost the capacity to feel humor."

It seems that those who attempt or commit suicide do so because they take themselves or their world too seriously. When life is severely out of balance, those who can't find anything to laugh about frequently want to end it.

Still, even here there is an occasional connection to humor. For example, one woman told me that laughter actually saved her life. One day she decided she would kill herself by jumping off a bridge. She walked out to the middle of the span, sat on the edge, and looked down. As she did, she noticed that she had worn a pair of brand-new, very expensive shoes. Suddenly she realized that if she jumped into the water her new shoes would be ruined. With this absurdly funny thought, instead of leaping forward into the river, she aborted her suicide when she fell backward with laughter.

WHO NOSE?

When my daughter, Sarah, was a teenager, she worked at a camp every summer. One year she asked if I would come and do a humor program for the counselors. I repeatedly said, "No."

In spite of my response, Sarah was persistent. Every summer she would ask if I would come and address the counselors. Every summer I would make some excuse why I could not—my busy schedule, my writing, the long drive, and so forth.

Then, one year, at a conference I attended, I heard a speaker give a powerful talk. At one point, he mentioned that teenagers have the highest suicide rate in this country. I thought about the teenage counselors Sarah asked me to address. I immediately phoned her and said, "When would you like me to come and speak?"

After the lengthy drive, I arrived at the camp and tried to find Sarah. She was not around at the time, but from the moment I stepped out of the car, everyone I met knew me. "Hello," they said, "you're Sarah's dad, aren't you?"

It wasn't until later that I learned that everyone knew who I was because, unbeknownst to me, Sarah had posted hundreds of small signs around the camp with my cartoon picture. The headline over it read, "Do you know this man?"

In my thirteen-year speaking career, I have never had such great prepublicity. Nor have I ever had such unusual accommodations—a cabin shared with two other counselors, a lumpy cot, holes in the screens, and bathroom facilities a quarter of a mile down the road.

The accommodations were less than ideal, the food was mediocre, and the fee was nil, but the experience was golden.

In the past, I have addressed fifteen hundred case managers at Opryland Hotel's grand ballroom, hundreds of hospice workers, who deal with death daily, and people with cancer and AIDS. But this is the speech I remember most.

I could not begin my talk until near 11 P.M.—yes, P.M.—after all the campers were put to bed and the counselors had free time for themselves. The room was packed with young, eager, but tired faces. They had been working since 6 A.M.

As I started to speak, I scanned the room in search of one counselor that I was concerned about. He was a friend of my daughter whom I had previously met. He was very shy, and from Sarah's description, frequently severely depressed.

I didn't see him in the crowded room and thought to myself that because of his depression, he probably chose not to attend my upbeat program. Then I spotted him hiding behind the couch. He would peer at me from time to time.

The speech went very well, and near midnight it ended with a standing ovation.

I didn't see Sarah's friend again until months later. Though he never wanted to chat much in the past, this time he was eager to share something. It seems that several days after my talk, things weren't going well at camp for him, so he decided to leave. Since he did not get along with his dad, he couldn't go home. So he left it up to fate and began hitchhiking. For most of the day, one car after another passed him by. He began to feel more and more depressed and deserted. He started to plan how he would kill himself. Then he put his hand in his pocket and discovered the clown nose he got at my talk. He put it on. Immediately someone stopped and gave him a ride.

"Maybe lightening up a bit can get me further than I thought," he told me. "Thank you, for coming to speak to us—and for saving my life."

Humor and Disasters

We're in pain, of course, but to cheer ourselves up, we get together and laugh from the bottom of our hearts. At any moment, we're scared. But at least this way, if there's another earthquake and I'm killed, I won't die alone.

—KUNIMASA NAKATA, after the Kobe, Japan, earthquake

There is an amusing tale I sometimes tell in my workshops that speaks of humor and disaster. It comes from the Jewish tradition. The story says that the world will come to an end in three days. In three days, everything will be deluged by water and everyone will drown.

After hearing this, the pope goes on television and says, "Don't worry, if you all turn to Christ, you will be saved."

The head of the Zen community also goes on TV and says, "Don't worry, if you put your faith in Buddha, you will be saved."

Then the head rabbi of Israel appears on TV and says, "Don't worry, folks, we have three days to learn how to live underwater."

Some people who have experienced natural disasters can relate to the above story. During the Midwest floods, for example, a partially submerged restaurant hung up a sign that read: "Waitress wanted. Must be able to swim underwater."

The following billboard signs were also spotted after the 1993 Midwest flooding:

Questions about the weather?
Call 1-800-NOAH

Welcome to Missouri,
the Row Me State
(Missouri is the Show Me State.)

The weather lately
gives a whole new meaning
to Roe vs. Wade

After a flood in Saint Louis, some creative soul hung up this sign: "Beach Front Property, Cheap." In Iowa, the *Des Moines Register* ran an "I'm a Floody Mess" contest. One entry from a farmer joked that he was going to sell corn "by the gallon." And after the cleanup began, the Chamber of Commerce ran ads that read: "Now Open for Business. No Wading."

The earthquake in California provided similar laughs. One mother, for example, who wanted to see if her son remembered the earthquake earlier that day, asked him, "What did we have this morning?" The child replied, "Cheerios and corn flakes."

And when the porch roof collapsed, one youngster came running out of the house yelling, "I didn't do it! I didn't do it! I didn't do it!"

As in the Midwest floods, signs played a big part in letting your neighbor know in an amusing way that you were okay. One person, for example, posted this sign on their earthquake-ravaged home: "House for rent. Some assembly required." Others spotted were "There goes the neighborhood" and (referring to both the earthquake and the subsequent fires) "Shake and Bake."

And finally, one newspaper reported that "moments after a part of the Bay Bridge had nearly collapsed on them, two house painters were sitting in their truck stunned, but in good humor. 'I want my dollar (toll) back,' said one." The reporter who wrote the article, Lisa Krieger, summed up why people joke in disasters: "It helps us gain control over our life: What scares us, we seek to make ridiculous. And what is ridiculous, can't hurt us."

After examining survivor humor associated with earthquakes, hurricanes, and firestorms, Sandy Ritz, Dr.Ph., found these types of humor in the four overlapping emotional phases of disasters:

1. *The Heroic Phase*

   If any humor occurs at this level, it is usually spontaneous. Ritz gives an example: "Two hikers, caught on the coast trail of Kauai when Hurricane Iniki struck, sang the theme song from *Gilligan's Island.* They kept up their spirits and dispelled their anxiety by reframing the situation in a comical format."

2. *The Honeymoon Phase*

   The humor here is positive and upbeat. It reflects recovery optimism. The example here comes from a T-shirt: "Landscaped by Iniki."

3. *The Disillusionment Phase*

   This stage resonates a feeling of disappointment and anger as agencies and community groups become less involved. Survivors feel isolated and pessimistic—and their humor reflects this. One example comes from another T-shirt; this one was produced after hurricane Andrew slammed the Florida coast. It read, "I survived Hurricane Andrew, but FEMA is killing me." (FEMA is the Federal Emergency Maintenance Association.)

4. *The Reconstruction Phase*

   The humor here may reflect a sense of community as people begin to rebuild and recover. For example, after two years of disasters in the southern California area, residents were heard remarking, "Los Angeles has four distinct seasons: Earthquake, Flood, Firestorm, and Mud Slide!"

Ritz notes that the type of humor a survivor uses or appreciates may depend on the phase of emotional recovery he or she is in. An important element here is that accessing the kind of humor a survivor is drawn to could be a useful tool in determining their mental health and their coping status.

I have found that life persists in the midst of destruction and, therefore, there must be a higher law than that of destruction.

—MAHATMA GANDHI

DISASTER JOKES

After any major disaster, jokes run rampant. They appear within minutes of a catastrophe. These so-called sick jokes travel around the world as people try to comprehend the immensity of the loss. This black humor, unlike the humor in Ritz's investigation, is most frequently created by those *not* directly connected to the disaster.

Alan Dundes, a professor of anthropology at the University of California at Berkeley, says that jokes of this kind provide an important emotional release valve. "Where there is anxiety," says Dundes, "there will be jokes to express that anxiety."

These jokes, which emerge from such disasters as earthquakes, hurricanes, airplane crashes, and nuclear accidents, are both comforting and confounding.

On the one hand, we find them tasteless—"How could you possibly say a thing like that?" On the other hand, in spite of our protest, we are eager to pass them along to others. The reason for their proliferation is that even in their harshness they unite people in their tragedy. We joke about the disaster because it is too difficult to discuss directly.

Examples of this kind of humor were heard:

• *After the Challenger shuttle explosion*
  "You know what *NASA* stands for?"
  "Need another seven astronauts."

• *After the TWA airplane crashed into the ocean*
  "What does *TWA* stand for?"
  "Tourists Washing Ashore."

• *After the World Trade Center bombing*
  "What's the charge for parking at the World Trade Center?"
  "An arm and a leg."

• *After the Chernobyl nuclear-power-plant disaster*
  "What do you serve with chicken Kiev?"
  "A black Russian."

• *And after the Three Mile Island crisis deepened*
  "What melts on the ground and not in your mouth?"
  "Hershey, Pennsylvania."

While sick jokes may offend, they also affirm. They remind us that for the survivor, life must go on. In spite of the overwhelming loss, if we can laugh about it, we know that "we'll get through this somehow."

THE final chapters of *The Courage to Laugh* look at the humor that is found just prior and just after someone has died. It examines the comical last wishes and humorous last words people have uttered as death was near. It also examines the humor found in planning for a funeral, during the funeral itself, and in the eulogies for the deceased. In addition, we look down the road after a loss at humor in the grieving process.

And finally, we examine the humorous and entertaining epitaphs used to honor loved ones, as well as the funny and fond memories that help keep loved ones alive.

Part III

Leave 'Em

Laughing

Chapter 12

Last Laughs

I want to come back as me.
— ED KOCH, former mayor of New York City

Last Wishes

VIRGINIA'S LAST REQUEST

In a book entitled *The Breast: An Anthology,* author Hanna-Ian Faraclas recounts a riotous tale about her mother's last request. Eleven months before her mother's death, Faraclas spent an entire day with her recording all of her last wishes in a notebook—information about the pallbearers, speakers, prayer givers, funeral home, grave marker, as well as details on the estate, insurance policies, bank accounts, and a list of people to whom her mother wanted to give her personal belongings. Faraclas was committed to carrying out her mother's desires to the fullest. Then it happened:

> Not quite a year had passed when I reached for the little notebook and placed it beside my plane ticket as I prepared to fly from Connecticut to Utah: my mother had died that morning. Twenty-four hours later I sat at a long dining table with many of my aunts and uncles (my mother was one of nine siblings) as they all took turns sharing memories and interesting stories of growing up on the Alberta prairie with their sister, Virginia. I listened and savored every word. One of my aunts having spent the pre-

vious week visiting my mother, related the experiences of the last days of my mother's life. Then she paused, and, looking directly at me, asked, "Do you know your mother had a last request?"

Secure in the belief that my notebook entries were complete, I asked which one she was referring to. According to my aunt this was a new wish, one my mother had discussed only with her the previous week. I was committed to carrying out all of my mother's wishes, but what was this new one? I looked to my aunt for illumination. Her face grew serious, and she said, "Your mother wants to be buried with 'falsies'!" Silence was followed by a roar of laughter, as surprise gave way to endearing humor.

Turning to my aunt I asked, "You do intend to carry out her wish, don't you?" She replied, "Of course not, don't be ridiculous." I was taken aback at her reluctance; a last wish is a last wish and I insisted that Virginia's be taken seriously. I was unable to persuade my aunt, who suddenly produced a set of foam rubber falsies—given to her by my mother, of course—and tossed them down the length of the dining table. She declared, "Okay, you do it!" as all heads turned to watch them heading straight toward me. I caught them, examined them briefly, then threw them right back to her. "No, you do it. She asked you." All heads now turned to watch my aunt catch the falsies. Again, she refused and volleyed once more. Falsies flew back and forth, with heads turning in unison to follow the action.

"She gave her dying wish to you," I said in a last ditch effort, as I caught the bosom boosters. Then, accepting my aunt's reluctance, conceded, "All right, I will do it. I intend to carry out her every last wish!" . . .

The following afternoon . . . we saw Virginia for the first time since her death. . . . After the reality of death took hold more fully, the aunts and uncles adjourned in nearby chairs to continue their reunion. With everyone engaged, I took the opportunity to get the "falsies" out of my bag and I stood beside my mother's body wondering how in the world I was going to get these things in the appropriate place, as she was already beautifully dressed in a gown that zipped down the back. I wasn't about to call the funeral director for help with this personal matter

Alone, and with difficulty, I attempted to lift the cowl neck line of my mother's dress and slide the soft rubber down her chest. Surprised I was, but also delighted, when my sweet aunt came to my side and together we placed the small shaped cups on her flatness. Shortly, two of my uncles joined us and offered the artistic commentary that only men can provide, "This one's too low." "That one's off to the side." "Now it's too high." "It looks like the breast of a young woman." "Yes, that's just right." And as a family, we all participated in the final arrangement of Virginia's last request.

....

I may not be in the greatest shape on my deathbed to utter the following zingers that I would love to pass on to those I've left behind. So, for now—and then—here are my last words:

Always get power steering.

Never give digoxin on Sunday.

Keep your kids off motorcycles, cigarettes, and booze.

Give insulin twice a day.

Drive a big car.

Keep out of jails and hospitals.

—O S C A R   L O N D O N , M . D . , *Kill as Few Patients as Possible*

....

THE LAST SUPPERS

The Living/Dying Project, in northern California, is an organization that works with terminally ill patients and their families. One of their newsletters contained this wonderfully warm and witty story written by project manager Laura Torbet:

Gail asked me and her closest friend Mariah to spend those final days with her. . . .

The second evening in the hospital, Mariah prepared a lavish "Last Supper," complete with polished silver, tablecloth, and a shameless excess of truffles. After the meal, her longtime Buddhist teacher arrived to do a final candlelight ritual with her. In a haze of satiety and love, we said our good-byes.

But Gail woke up again the next morning. No one was more shocked—and disoriented—than she; this was not according to plan. So what could we do but have another "last" supper? Mustering her energy and spirit to join in life for another day, she spearheaded the menu plans for another decadent meal . . . [and] we again said our good-byes.

But Gail didn't go anywhere, and woke to another day on earth. Now it was getting tougher for her to maintain her carefully calibrated readiness to die. Humor—most of it Gail's—saved the day. She made us promise to take her out at dawn and shoot her if she wasn't dead by daybreak. . . .

Gail lived for four more days . . . each day she was pulled back into the world she was so prepared to leave; each day her disappointment at still being alive was profound. Like a trooper, she would rally with an increasingly outlandish—and increasingly hard to fulfill—wish for some special treat, which she would wait for with a true sensualist's anticipation: a piece of St. Honore cake, quince sorbet, the kind of chocolate truffle that is hard on the outside, but soft on the inside. For Gail, I think dreaming up these exotic treats was a way of making bearable the additional day of unwanted life, a last pleasure she could take in the face of her disappointments. Fulfilling these demands was the only way for Mariah and me to give Gail comfort as she waited for death to claim her.

In the end, Gail's last supper consisted of *dulce de leche,* like the one she'd eaten while traveling with her father in Mexico, at a bar where the dancers balanced pineapples on their heads. The next afternoon, in a smiling twilight of semi-consciousness, her last words were: " . . . it was a white cake . . . with soft swirly white icing. . . . There were green leaves . . . translucent, the color green of the gorgeous dress Felice . . . wore at your birthday party." For Mariah and me, it was the last of many laughs.

THE LAST PICTURES

A week before one young man died, he asked his mother to bring him all his slide carousels. He rearranged the slides, slipped in a few others, and made his mother promise to show them and read his commentary to his family and friends after his death.

He truly left them laughing. He had arranged the slides in a hilarious sequence with an equally funny commentary. In addition, near the end of the slide presentation, he put some NASA slides of the manned flights to the moon showing the spacecraft moving into the heavens and getting progressively smaller as it got farther and farther away.

Last Words

....

This wallpaper is terrible! One of us has to go!

—OSCAR WILDE'S LAST WORDS

....

YOU GO FIRST

"If there were two things that were true about my dad," Terry Brewer, speaker and humorist, told me, "it was, first, that he always used humor to bring perspective. And second, he was scared to death of dying. So to me it was ironic, or at least fitting, that he used humor to deal with the inevitable."

Brewer said, "As the elder son, it fell to me to talk to my dad about his impending death. Even though it was awkward for me, when I knew the end was near, I went into his hospital room one afternoon and asked him if he was afraid to die. He nodded and whispered, 'A little.' So I immediately tried to bring him some comfort.

"I reminded him that we were from a strong Christian family and that he had raised us to understand that belief in God would mean life in the hereafter. So I smiled and said, 'Well, you know, Dad, we are all going to be in heaven someday.'

"Suddenly my dad's eyes opened and caught mine. Then he signaled with his hand for me to come closer. I really thought that this was it, that this was going to be the moment when all of his knowledge and wisdom would be imparted to his son. But as I got closer, he looked at me and said, 'Well, then, you go first.' "

WHO KILLED J.R.?

In his book *Flying Without Wings,* Arnold Beisser, M.D., writes about one woman's final words:

> Some young friends told me about their mother's death. She was
> a wonderful woman who died heroically after a long, painful, and
> eroding cancer. The family spent as much time with her as pos-

sible, and felt the tragedy of her suffering and impending death deeply. One day, when she was close to dying, she opened her eyes to speak. They leaned close to hear what might be her final words to them. She whispered, "Who killed J.R.?" (referring to the popular television show *Dallas*). The family members, having expected some profound deathbed statement, began to laugh. The woman, who had not laughed in many weeks, joined with them in what is now recalled as a beautiful final moment together.

Either I'm dead or my watch has stopped.

—GROUCHO MARX'S LAST WORDS

I'VE CHANGED MY MIND

Naomi Rhode is a past president of the National Speakers Association, and with her husband, Jim, owner of a large company. Rhode told me a poignantly funny story about her mom's death. She began, "In the cold, sub-zero weather of northern Minnesota, I sat with my mother in the Two Harbors Hospital while she was dying. I was twenty-three years old, and losing a treasure of my heart. Ellen Reed was an incredible woman! Wise, loving, gentle, kind—a mentor. After losing my father, at age thirteen, this foreboding loss of my mother was almost incomprehensible. She had been one of the first people to have open heart surgery, and had survived ten years after that experience. Even that 'magic of medicine' had now given way to entropy, and her death seemed inevitable."

Rhode continued, "Saturday afternoon she spent hours with my brother and with me reminiscing. Then with a sigh, she died. There was no breathing, no pulse, and the nurse confirmed that she was gone. Moments passed, as we stood by her lifeless body trying to silently cope with our grief. Then," said Rhode, "her eyes opened, she smiled gently, and these words came from her mouth: 'I changed my mind!' "

Ellen Reed eventually died, but Rhode came to realize that "yes, amidst the tragedy there was that moment of humor."

Guru Baba Meher died in 1969, but because he lived in silence, his last words were actually spoken in 1925. They were: "Don't worry, be happy."

Last Writes

....

Friend! for your epitaphs I'm griev'd,
Where still so much is said,
One half will never be believ'd,
The other never read.
— ALEXANDER POPE

....

Pope was right. Much of what is written as epitaphs is never read and soon forgotten. But the deceased who lie under tombstone wit have achieved a certain immortality, as their epitaphs are often quoted in various publications. So once again humor triumphs—those who have passed on haven't been passed over.

"The object of an epitaph," according to the *Churchyard Handbook,* "is to identify the resting place of the mortal remains of a dead person." Therefore, the handbook states, it should "record only such information as is reasonably necessary for that purpose." Fortunately for the deceased, whose memory is immortalized on headstone humor, those who wrote the epitaphs did not pay much attention to the handbook.

Many old epitaphs immortalize the deceased by poking fun at their names, which, of course, those buried beneath the tombstone no longer need.

Here lies Ann Mann.
She lived an old maid
but died an old Mann.

Sacred to the memory of Lettuce Manning
Oh, cruel death
To satisfy thy palate,
Cut down our Lettuce
To make a salad

When people are ill they come to I.
I physics, bleeds, and sweats 'em.
Sometimes they live, sometimes they die:
What's that to I? I Letsome.

Dr. I. Letsome

A more recent name-play tombstone in Arizona reads:

Here
Lies
Lester Moore
Four slugs
From a 44
No Les
No more

Poking fun at the profession of the deceased is also used as a variation on name play. One of the briefest epitaphs in this vein is on a gardener's epitaph. It reads: "Transplanted."

Another, for a dentist, reads:

Stranger! Approach this spot with gravity!
John Brown is filling his last cavity.

Some used the tombstone to advertise:

Here lies Jane Smith
wife of Thomas Smith,
marble cutter. This
monument was erected by
her husband as a
tribute to her memory
and a specimen of his work.
Monuments of the same
style 350 dollars.

While others use it to apologize:

Here lies a father of 29.
There would have been more
but he didn't have time.

Another device to add humor to headstones is to poke fun at the way someone died. Here is an example found in an Enosburg, Vermont, graveyard:

Here Lies the body of our Anna
Done to death by a banana.
It wasn't the fruit that laid her low
But the skin of the thing that made her go.

While most of the funny grave markers were intentionally written, every once in a while, the humor is unintentional. One tombstone I spotted in an old cemetery in California gold-rush country stood out because of the stonecutter's poor spelling. It read: "Gone to be an Angle."

When Oliver died, he and Kathy had been married for fifteen years. Kathy was grief-stricken. She kept saying, "What use is there in living without Oliver?" In fact, she had this inscription engraved on his tombstone: "The Light Of My Life Has Gone Out."

Two years later Kathy met John and fell in love with him. She was bothered about the inscription on Oliver's tombstone. Finally she had a phrase added to the inscription: "The Light Of My Life Has Gone Out, But I Struck Another Match."

—JIM KEELAN, *Laugh Your Way to Health*

Both comedians and writers have used the epitaph as an art form to show off their skill and their wit. Perhaps the best known are the words of W. C. Fields, who wanted this on his cemetery marker: "On the whole, I'd rather be in Philadelphia."

Here, in jest or in earnest, are what other celebrities have said they want on their tombstone:

Film star Constance Bennett: "Do not disturb."

Comedy writer Goodman Ace: "No flowers please, I'm allergic."

Actor Paul Newman: "Here lies Paul Newman, who died a failure because his eyes turned brown."

Dr. Albert Schweitzer:
If cannibals should ever catch me,
I hope they will say:
"We have eaten Dr. Schweitzer,
And he was good to the end,
And the end wasn't bad."

Comedian Johnny Carson: "I'll be right back."
Comedian Joan Rivers: "Wait—can we talk?"
*Mel Blanc, the voice of Bugs Bunny, Daffy Duck, and a host of other cartoon
   characters:* "That's all, folks!"

Writer Dorothy Parker often wrote cynically but humorously about
both life and death. Her poem on suicide was quoted earlier. Here, from a
series of epitaphs about people with different professions, is one entitled
"The Actress":

> *Her name, cut clear upon this marble cross,*
> *Shines, as it shone when she was still on earth;*
> *While tenderly the mild, agreeable moss*
> *Obscures the figures of her date of birth.*

....

For Sale: One used tombstone. Splendid opportunity for family named
Dingle.

—MADISON (WIS.) *Capital Times*

....

THE TOMBSTONE TEST

Writing our own tombstone can be a wonderful way of ascertaining how
we want to be remembered in this world after we are gone. In a delightful
book entitled *Life Is Uncertain . . . Eat Dessert First!,* authors Sol Gordon and
Harold Brecher suggest taking the Tombstone Test:

> Ask yourself, "If I died tomorrow, how would I want my
> tombstone to read? That I made a mound of money? That I
> gave my all to becoming successful? That I enjoyed life to the
> fullest?"
>
> If you want to be remembered as a loving person, some-
> what successful, who never lost sight of the importance of bring-
> ing happiness to yourself and others, it's not too soon to start
> restructuring your life to that end.
>
> Read the obituary columns occasionally, and you'll be
> alerted to how trivial someone's press-worthy achievements seem
> after death.

One example that comes readily to mind: When the "pioneer of Tex-Mex cuisine" died, the obituary column noted his two main achievements in life—having created a crisp taco shell and smothering his enchiladas in sour cream.

MONUMENTAL FUN

Modern technological advances, such as color computer-enhanced laser etching, have literally changed the face of tombstones and allowed more leeway for humor. "Ten years ago it was nothing but Bibles, roses, and crosses," says one monument builder. But today you can find such things as dancing elephants, golf clubs, and beer cans on grave markers. One tombstone, for example, has a picture of a Visa card etched on it with the words "Charge it" above the card and "Send the bill to heaven" below the card.

Someone who was cremated chose "I made an ash out of myself" on their tombstone. Another very contemporary marker reads: "Be excellent to each other, and party on, dudes." And a third humorously warns: "Look out, heaven, here she comes."

Not only do some epitaphs, like the ones above, evoke laughter, but sometimes the tombstones themselves exhibit a bizarre sense of humor. For example:

—The headstone of a former concert pianist is a twenty-five-ton black granite grand piano.
—One woman chose a pair of oversized playing cards and some dice as an offbeat headstone for her avid-gambler husband.
—A man who was killed in an auto accident has a headstone flanked by two parking meters that read, "Expired."

The electronic age we live in has also opened up new ways of being remembered. One company, for example, has invented a talking tombstone. Instead of merely chiseled words on stone, you can actually leave your voice behind saying those words. Guaranteed for two generations, this solar-powered device can record up to a ninety-minute message.

But you need not go to such extremes. A simpler, less expensive, do-it-yourself talking epitaph can be accomplished via videotape. Below, for example, is one postdeath videotaped message created by a woman in her forties who left her entire estate to her husband:

> *Don't go to Vegas, or play with stock,*
> *Or drink much after six o'clock.*
> *Or party far into the night,*
> *You'll join me if you don't live right.*
> *And sports cars and funny hats,*
> *You're really much too old for that.*
> *And please, when all my songs are sung.*
> *Don't fall for someone cute and young.*

In the end, everything is a gag.

—CHARLIE CHAPLIN

COMFORT LEFT FROM THE HEREAFTER

There is a popular poem by an unknown author that goes:

> *Do not stand at my grave and weep;*
> *I am not here. I do not sleep.*
> *I am a thousand winds that blow.*
> *I am the diamond glints on snow.*
> *I am the sunlight on ripened grain.*
> *I am the gentle autumn's rain.*
> *When you awaken in the morning's hush,*
> *I am the swift uplifting rush*
> *Of quiet birds in circled flight.*
> *I am the soft stars that shine at night.*
> *Do not stand at my grave and cry:*
> *I am not there. I did not die.*

To this anonymous poet's words, I would add:
I am the comfort left from the hereafter.
I am the soothing song of laughter.

Chapter 13

Celebration of Loss

To weep too much for the dead is to affront the living.
—OLD PROVERB

One day, while walking down the street, I noticed that someone had taken the FUNERAL sign from a funeral-car procession, cut it apart, and rearranged the letters. The sign now read, REAL FUN.

Certainly funerals are not real fun, but as evidenced in this chapter, humor can be found while making the funeral arrangements, at the funeral itself, and in the eulogies for the deceased. Anyone who has ever tried to stop laughing during a funeral when something funny has struck them knows that there can be laughter at a funeral—sometimes lots of it.

Amidst the crying and sadness at a death there often comes a time when the solemnity of the event shifts to celebration. For many cultures, the funeral is cause for members of the family to gather together in a group. The funeral becomes an important social event. Friends, relatives, and neighbors who have not seen one another for years, or perhaps never met at all, are suddenly thrown together not only to reminisce about the dead but also to catch up on the events of the living. These postdeath celebrations are important events that bring the realization that life does indeed go on. In essence, they remind us that "we have our family, our friends, and our community. Let's celebrate while we can."

Funeral Arrangements

While she was shopping for a casket for her deceased mother, an eager funeral home salesman turned a grief-stricken woman's anguish to laughter. When he assured her that the top-of-the-line coffin had a century-long waterproof guarantee, she wondered aloud, "Who will be around in a hundred years to see if it is leaking?"

GOOD BUY

We don't expect to find humor in arranging for a funeral; nonetheless, it can be found here too. For example, Rick Segel, owner of a women's apparel store in Massachusetts, told me about two humorous funeral-planning incidents that took place in his heavily populated Italian neighborhood.

"People would come into our store on a regular basis to buy dresses in which to lay out the deceased," Segel said. "They always asked for the same thing—long sleeves, high neck, and in blue. And they always told me the same thing—'No pink. The casket is lined in pink.'

"One day three sisters come into the store, and I could tell that they were picking out a dress for their deceased mother. One sister picked up a dress and remarked, 'That's so beautiful. That looks like mother. That is just so perfect.'

"The second sister, the sister of reason, said, 'Are you crazy? That dress is six hundred and ninety-five dollars. We are not going to spend that kind of money to lay Mom out.'

"The third sister, the compromiser, said, 'Oh, let's go ahead and get it. After all, we're not going to have to buy her a Mother's Day present anymore.'

"So," says Segel, "they bought the six hundred and ninety-five dollar dress."

In another incident associated with funeral arrangements, Segel told me:

It's a busy Saturday afternoon in the store and I'm taking in the money as fast as I can. All of a sudden, a woman walks up to the counter with the ugliest dress in the store. This dress is so ugly that it was a veteran of seven sidewalk sales. The fabric was a double-knit polyester in an awful peach color with four G clefs embroidered across the breast in matching fake pearls.

Originally the dress sold for $249; now it was marked down to $15!

Just as I thought I was finally going to get rid of the dress, the customer said, "Look, one sleeve is dirty."

So I tried to clean the spot, but it only got worse.

"I'm so sorry, ma'am," I said. "I can't sell you the dress. It's too badly damaged."

"You don't understand. That dress was for my sister to be laid out," the woman said.

"Well, I guess she's going to have to go to eternity wearing something else," I said.

"You don't understand," she insisted. "My sister has always been very frugal."

"So," I replied.

"So, if you mark the dress down to nine dollars, I'll tell you what I'll do. I'll tell the undertaker to put one arm over the other. Then my sister will rest in peace knowing that she got a good buy!"

"Sold," I said.

....

Before she died, one woman wrote very specific instructions for her funeral service. The woman, who was never married, informed the undertaker, "I don't want any male pallbearers. They wouldn't take me out when I was alive; I don't want them to take me out when I'm dead!"

....

JUMPING FOR JOY

Dianne Fidelibus, a woman from Bexley, Ohio, told me about an experience that occurred when she and her sister were planning their father's funeral.

At the funeral home, while going over the details, Fidelibus said to her sister, "Oh, my gosh, we haven't even thought about who is going to be the pole-vaulters." As the funeral director started to snicker, Fidelibus realized what she had said, and all three of them burst out laughing. But the laughter didn't stop there. Her father was a member of the Veterans of Foreign Wars. "So every time these old VFW guys would offer to be a pallbearer, my sister and I would laugh, thinking, 'I wonder how high he can jump,' " says Fidelibus.

Three and a half years later, Fidelibus's mother, Betty Williams, was diagnosed with terminal lung cancer. At one point, her mother said, "I don't care what you do, but you have to promise that you will have as much fun planning my funeral as you did your dad's. And," she insisted, "I want my very own pole-vaulters."

"I feel so blessed," shares Fidelibus, "that the moment we needed some humor to pull us all together, it was there."

Cohen approaches the secretary of the burial society.

"I'm here because my wife is dead, and I have to arrange for her funeral."

"Your wife is dead?" asks the secretary. "How can that be? We buried your wife two years ago!"

"No, no," says Cohen. "That was my first wife. This was my second."

"Really?" says the secretary. "I didn't know you got married again. Mazel Tov!"

—WILLIAM NOVAK AND MOSHE WALDOKS,
The Big Book of Jewish Humor

THEY SHOOT MOMS, DON'T THEY?

Anne DiScarina's uncle died suddenly, so the entire family went to the funeral home to purchase a headstone. While they were there, the funeral sales director talked the entire family—Anne, her mother, and her two aunts—into buying headstones for themselves.

"I'll give you a better deal if you buy them all at once," the salesman said. "And while you are at it," he continued, "how about putting your names on it? After all, if you are going to have the guy come to do one, why not do them all?"

Everyone agreed.

Then the salesman turned to DiScarina and asked her how old her aunt and mother were. She told him that they were in their late seventies. The salesman suggested, "Well, they are probably not going to live forever. Why don't we inscribe the number nineteen on the headstone? Then we'll just have to chip in the rest of the year when they die."

Again, DiScarina agreed. She signed the papers and left.

Years later, DiScarina and her mother were sitting on the beach. "I don't know how we got to talking about dying and stuff," she says, "but I turned to my mother and remarked, 'You know, Ma, I was just thinking. If you don't die by December 31, 1999, I'm going to have to shoot you!' "

Without missing a beat, her mother asked, "Oh, don't you think they can erase the nineteen?"

DiScarina answered, "No problem. If not, I'll just put '1999 plus'!"

Memorable Memorials

A young, inexperienced preacher was conducting his first funeral. He gestured to the body lying in the coffin and declared, "What we have here is only the shell. The nut is already gone."

In questioning people about how they wanted others to react to their death, I found that most people desired their survivors to celebrate their demise rather than mourn their passing. After their death, they wanted people to party and have a good time.

Funerals can be a celebration for the joyousness of a life lived rather than for a life that is no longer. There can be a sharing by everyone who knew the deceased rather than the reciting of a few meaningless words spoken by someone who did not. Perhaps, then, a memorial to the dead would allow for more humor to emerge.

REVERENT ABOUT LIFE

"Funerals, American-Style, are not supposed to be funny," writes author Robert Fulghum in his book *Uh-Oh.* "Death must be treated with solemn dignity. . . . However. Like the careless shape of life itself, funerals often do not work out quite according to plan," says Fulghum. "As a parish minister involved backstage in more than two hundred funerals, I can testify that, like weddings, funerals have a soap-opera quality that can get out of hand and turn into comic operas worthy of Gilbert and Sullivan."

Another member of the clergy, the Reverend John Snyder, knows exactly what Fulghum is talking about. One of his most memorable funerals was conducted for a man who weighed hundreds and hundreds of pounds. The man was so heavy that a tractor had to be used to move the specially constructed coffin to the graveside. Everything went well until an unforeseen balancing problem occurred. When the family arrived, the coffin started to slip. As if straight out of a Laurel and Hardy movie, the coffin slid—not into the grave, but down the hill. At first people were aghast. But soon a few smiles appeared, followed by snickers, and then lots of loud belly laughs.

"Thank God for these real-life accidents that keep us from the boredom of perfection," says Fulghum. One year he addressed the annual convention of the National Hospice Organization and delighted the audience with such a story:

> My first year in the ministry, I was twenty-four "wise" years old. I thought I knew everything I needed to know about being a minister, and I did not have to ask anybody's advice. . . .
>
> This is why I so readily and easily agreed to help a lady scatter the ashes of Harry, her husband, from an airplane. I expected the whole thing to be a piece of cake. . . .
>
> I wore my brand new clerical gown for the occasion, and off we went. At about 5,000 feet, when the plane got over the bay, the pilot held the cockpit door open while I removed the urn lid, preparing to toss the ashes. Suddenly, though, the slipstream filled the cockpit, and ol' Harry blew everywhere, covering everything and everybody. . . .
>
> Eventually, I wrote an addition to the [minister's] manual which reads like this: "After filling the cockpit with ashes, we returned to the airport, found the janitor, and vacuumed the deceased. Special note: It is very important to use a new cleaner bag." Fortunately, the widow was calm, cool, and collected about the whole thing. "This will be funny . . . some day," she said.
>
> She went off to her car with Harry's ashes there in the vacuum cleaner. I don't know what finally happened to him, but I did wonder about what else might be with him in the bag. And I have a sense of pity for whoever poured him out the next time.
>
> It is nice we can laugh at such things. You see, I am not terribly reverent about death. But I am reverent about life. And one of the ways you know you are alive and well is that you can laugh, even about something that seems so sorrowful as death."

A funeral should be a place you laugh, you know. Those who understand the faith know that death is not the end.
—THE REVEREND DOUG ADAMS, United Church of Christ

ALL FALL DOWN

In *The Healing Power of Humor,* I quoted a column by Ann Landers that described how she and her equally famous sister, who writes the "Dear Abby" column, convulsed with laughter at their mother's funeral. I've since come across a column by Abigail Van Buren herself dealing with laughter at funerals. She told the letter writer, "It should comfort you to know that my mail is filled with letters from others who also got the giggles at a funeral." Then she published the note she had received:

> After reading the letter about the two grown men (cousins) who got the giggles during the funeral service of their uncle, I had to write and tell you what happened at my Grammy's funeral.
>
> The minister told everyone to stand for the eulogy and prayer, and that's when the giggling and snickering began. Soon, the minister was giggling and snickering along with the rest of the mourners. Guess what started it all? It seems that when Grampy stood up, his pants fell to his ankles, and he was so deep in prayer he didn't bother to pull up his pants until after the eulogy was over. After the funeral, everyone gathered at my mother's house where one of my uncles said, "Well, Dad sure got the last laugh on Mom!" That funny episode broke the tension and made Grammy's death a little less painful.

It is well known that one is inclined to laugh at funerals more readily, more loudly—indeed, more hysterically—than on any other occasion. This is caused by our desire to overcome fear and death, and has nothing to do with the question whether death is a legitimate subject of humour.

—GEORGE MIKES, *Humour in Memoriam*

KISSES AND ONIONS

In her exposé of the funeral industry, author Jessica Mitford questioned the appropriateness of ceremonies that go to great lengths to display a lifeless corpse. Perhaps the time has come for us to give a second thought to what memorial would be most fitting to the deceased rather than abiding by the elaborate wastefulness and regimentation that the funeral industry often dictates.

Funeral homes, for example, may not always be the appropriate place for a service. They are usually unfamiliar surroundings that hold little or no meaning for the bereaved other than perhaps providing a large enough space for friends and relatives to gather.

More hospitable places would be more conducive to people relaxing and opening up to the possibility of more humor. In my first book, for example, I talk about a funeral appropriately set in a nightclub because that is where the person was employed and that was where his creative energy was.

The Natural Death Care Project in northern California is an organization that is helping people change the way funerals are conducted. Jerri Lyons, its founder, gave me two examples of memorial services in which everyone took an active part. As a result, they became more meaningful and less somber.

Lyons said, "The casket was a plain pine box which the deceased had hand-stenciled before her death. Friends put the closed box on the middle of the floor and made a beautiful autumn arrangement around it with mirrors, ribbons, leaves, and lace. Then they spread lots of candy kisses, the deceased's favorite, all around the mirrors and the lace. At the burial, mourners took handfuls of candy kisses and tossed them into the grave.

"Another family used a simple cardboard box for cremation but decorated it with colored pens. On it, they told the story of the deceased's life. There was, for example, a picture of a truck [because he was a truck driver] with 'Keep on Trucking' boldly written beside it and 'Go, Big Red' because he was a Nebraska football fan. There was also lots of red onions, which the deceased liked a lot."

Lyons says that decorating a coffin serves a double purpose. It provides a fun and meaningful way to memorialize the deceased and it is an active way in which friends and loved ones can participate in an event to help their healing.

....

Oh, lay me down in Forest Lawn in a silver casket,
Put golden flowers over my head in a silver basket.
Let the Drum and Bugle corps blow Taps while cannons roar,
Let sixteen liveried employees pass out souvenirs from the funeral store.

I want to go simply when I go,
They'll give me a simple fun'ral there I know.

With a casket lined in fleece and fireworks spelling out "Rest in Peace."
Oh, take me when I'm gone to Forest Lawn.

—TOM PAXTON

....

REAL FUN?

In his book *Humor: God's Gift,* author Tal Bonham tells this brief story of one man's plans for his own funeral:

> I like the way Catholic priest James G. O'Malley faced the pos-
> sibility of death when he was informed that cancer would allow
> him to live only about six more weeks. He decided to arrange his
> own funeral service and to share it with his friends and family.
>
> O'Malley, who had already undergone five operations
> for cancer, sent letters and telegrams to his friends and family say-
> ing, "You are cordially invited to the wake of Rev. James G.
> O'Malley at Philadelphia Naval Hospital."
>
> The "corpse" had a marvelous time at his wake. He shook
> hands with his friends, hugged and kissed their wives, shared hu-
> morous stories, and insisted that his friends follow the tradition
> of making speeches praising him. Among those present was his
> surprised doctor.
>
> O'Malley laughed throughout the entire wake and said
> good-bye to each of his friends with a big smile on his face. That
> was back in 1972, when O'Malley was an air force chaplain.
> Now, over sixty years of age, he is still laughing.

Humorous Eulogies

They say such nice things about people at their funerals. It is a shame that I
am going to miss mine by only a few days.

—GARRISON KEILLOR

When we think of a eulogy, usually humor does not come to mind. We think instead of a somber speech praising someone who has died. Yet two researchers have found that humor can be beneficial in eulogies because it increases the credibility of the speaker. What was most surprising about the findings, however, was that even inappropriate humor did not significantly hurt the speaker's credibility.

I am not suggesting that we add humor, inappropriate or otherwise, to a eulogy just to increase the speaker's credibility, but a few fond anecdotes about the deceased's life are appropriate, and often welcomed, as a counterbalance to the somberness of the event.

GRANDMA FRIEDA'S EULOGY

Glenn Rockowitz, an extremely funny man and founder of The Best Medicine, a company that promotes the therapeutic value of humor, shared with me the eulogy he gave for his grandmother. Here is a portion of the memorial speech for Grandma Frieda:

> All these thoughts [I'm having today] center around one central experience in our relationship with each other—laughing. I can even hear her now throughout all this chaos. She would be very honored to know about all of those people who responded sympathetically to the news of her death. I'd like to share some of those letters and thoughts with you now.
>
> First, this excerpt from a letter from the Prime Minister of Sri Lanka: "On behalf of all the citizens of my rather humble country, I would like to offer my sincere condolences on the loss of your grandmother Frieda Rockowitz. We are very sorry for your personal loss. On the other hand, we cannot offer enough gratitude for your grandmother's most generous gift to all peoples of Sri Lanka. After defrosting Frieda's freezer, we have found that there is enough food to feed each and every one of our citizens for well over three full months. For that we will be eternally grateful. Although we did receive several letters from some of our remote villages stating that 'the brisket was a little tough,' and that the soup marked 'Melvin's bris' did 'tend to repeat on us,' we were as a whole satisfied with the lot. . . ."
>
> Above all, Grandma's death brought tremendous happiness to only one person—my Grandpa Herman. For over five years now, he had been sitting patiently at the Big-Dinner-Table-Above waiting to eat. . . . This will be his first meal and his first BM in a very, very long time. I'll never forget the time Grandma called my father up to tell him not to worry—that ol' Gramps was "back in the saddle" and having a BM every morning at eight o'clock like clockwork. What she neglected to tell any of us was that he didn't get out of bed until nine. . . .
>
> Grandma always said that just because you shed light on a

situation doesn't necessarily mean you take a situation lightly. And I do NOT take this situation lightly. I loved my Grandma more than any of you could possibly imagine, and I miss her deeply already. I know she would laugh now as she did constantly throughout the last two weeks we spent together in the nursing home. I only wish that I can give to my grandchildren what Grandma has given to me—so much wisdom, strength, laughter and joy. And I am sure that one day, my grandchildren will be standing over my grave and saying those magical words I have waited a lifetime to hear: "What?!! All he left me was an ottoman?!!"

You will live with me forever, Grandma.

Two ships sailed in a harbor: one going out on a voyage, the other coming into port. People cheered the ship going out, but the ship sailing in was hardly noticed. Seeing this, a wise man remarked, "Do not rejoice for a ship sailing out to sea, for you do not know what terrible dangers it may encounter. Rejoice rather for the ship that has reached shore, bringing its passengers safely home."

And so it is in the world. When a child is born, all rejoice; when someone dies, all weep. But it makes just as much sense, if not more, to rejoice at the end of a life as at the beginning. For no one can tell what events await a newborn child, but when a mortal dies he has successfully completed a journey.

—THE TALMUD

AUNTIE RITA'S EULOGY

Rick Segel, the dress store owner, told me a humorous story about his Aunt Rita and her unusual request for her eulogy.

One day Auntie Rita (or as Boston-based Segel says, *Ountie Rita*) gathered her large family around and told them that she had two weeks to live. Then she planned the entire funeral—the food, the service, and even the eulogy, which she insisted Segel perform.

She also informed him that it had better be funny. "I want people should laugh," she said.

So Segel wrote the speech and showed it to his aunt the next day. She liked it but added more humorous material and had Segel practice it in front of her every day.

Four and a half weeks later, Auntie Rita was still alive.

One day, with most of her strength gone, she pulled Segel close to her and whispered in his ear, "I told everyone I only had two weeks to live. But you know, you were never such a good student. I figured you needed extra time to get the eulogy right so I hung on a little longer. Now that you have it perfect, it's time for me to go."

That night Auntie Rita died in her sleep.

The next day Segel delivered the eulogy. He knew he could get the laughs, but his biggest fear was that he would not be able to meet his Auntie Rita's expectation. At the end of the speech, after Segel recited all the funny stories, she had wanted him to raise both arms in the air and with tears flowing say, "Auntie Rita, I'm going to miss you."

After having practiced for so many weeks, Segel was afraid that the tears would not come. At the end of the speech, however, he raised his hands high in the air, said, "Auntie Rita, I'm going to miss you," and the tears did indeed flow, along with a great big smile on his face.

....

They say you shouldn't say nothing about the dead unless it's good. He's dead. Good.

—MOMS MABLEY

....

THE WAY YOU GET THROUGH THESE THINGS

Al McCree is a professional speaker and entertainer from Nashville, Tennessee. We discussed the joyous memorial service for his father, who had passed away less than two weeks before we spoke.

McCree said, "My father was a remarkable man, who was very active with his family, his business, his community, and his church. In planning his funeral service, I wanted to cover all of these areas. So I told my brother that we could do the service as a family and each speak about the different aspects of Dad's life."

When McCree and his family were sitting around brainstorming about what to say in the eulogy, the humor began. "I remember when Dad loaned us all money," McCree started. And then his sister chimed in, "And you know it was always at a very favorable interest—for him."

At the memorial service, McCree recalls, "Mom slipped the organist a copy of 'I'm a Rambling Wreck from Georgia Tech and a Hell of an Engineer' because Pop was an alumnus of Georgia Tech and a big fan." When that was played, says McCree, it immediately set the tone for a lighthearted service.

McCree's sister spoke first. One of her opening comments that got a laugh was, "Pop thought Mom hung the moon—even though he did tell her how to hang it." Then, when it was McCree's turn, he told the crowd that his dad would not be on a committee of which he wasn't the president. Knowing his dad well, the crowd laughed when McCree added, "He was a chief, he was not an Indian."

The humor that occurred at McCree's father's memorial may not have been the fall-down-laughing-in-the-aisle type. Joke telling would have been inappropriate. The humor that was used, however, evolved out of recollections from various aspects of the deceased's life. It was heartfelt and fitting.

McCree made several salient points about what had turned out to be, in his words, "a joyous memorial service."

One point was that survivors need not be particularly funny to conduct a humorous eulogy. "None of us," noted McCree, "are what you'd call naturally humorous or practical jokers. We were just seeking stories about Pop, and a lot of what people remembered was amusing."

One of the most important points McCree made was how much the retelling and remembering the humor of his father's memorial service helped him with the grief process. "It's good for me still to go over the service again with you," he said. "I mean, that's the way you get through these things."

Chapter 14

Mirth and Mourning

When people are merry and dance, it sometimes happens
that they catch hold of someone who is sitting outside and
grieving, pull him into the round, and make him rejoice
with them. The same happens in the heart of one who re-
joices; grief and sorrow draw away from him, but it is special virtue to pursue them with courage and to draw grief
into gladness, so that all the strength of sorrow may be
transformed into joy.

—HASIDIC TEACHING,
IN MARTIN BUBER, *Ten Rungs*

Grief Relief

Yes, it is difficult to deal with the loss of a loved one. Yes, it may seem like
it is the darkest time of our life. Still, if we look, there are lighter moments
among the dark ones. Sometimes they are few and far between, but they are
there. They are there to get us through the night, and if we are able to survive—and we must, after a loss, or else we are contributing to doubling that
loss—we must be willing to let some of those tiny rays of lightness in.

In his book *A Laughing Place,* Christian Hageseth III, M.D., touches on
the issue of laughter and loss. He says that "appropriate laughter while re-
calling the happy times is humor's role in human grief."

Hageseth concurs that laughter in the death-and-dying process "is not
neurotic and it is not irreverent. The use of humor in this way allows for
healing and the recovery of the capacity to love again—and to laugh again."

Learning to laugh after a loss means being compassionate with yourself and the world around you. The moment you are too hard on yourself, you lose the ability to laugh. You can learn to laugh the way you once did, but it takes time. Just as a baby must learn to crawl before it walks, and walk before it runs, so too, you can slowly learn to laugh again. And when you do, you know you are beginning to embrace life again.

The stories shared in this chapter illustrate how humor helped heal mourners' grief and how mirthful memories helped loved ones become immortal.

WE'VE GOT TO STOP MEETING LIKE THIS

"When I was twenty-six, my father passed away suddenly. He had a heart attack—it was his first and his last," Jeff Davidson, a colleague and professional speaker, told me. "That happened on February 17, 1977. Then, about eighteen months later," Davidson said, "my older sister, who was thirty-one years old, also died suddenly. In this case, she had a thrombosis, a blood clot.

"We were stunned when my father passed away because he was only sixty. Then, eighteen months later, to have another member of the family die, who was only thirty-one, puts you in a different realm altogether."

Davidson continues, "My sister lived in California at the time, I lived in Washington, and my mother lived in Connecticut. I flew home to be with the rest of the family. When my brother arrived, for some reason, I instinctively said to him, 'We've got to stop meeting like this!'

"I don't know why I said that. It was humorous for both my brother and myself, just for that moment. It didn't necessarily help with the grief that was coming, but for some reason, for that little moment, that one phrase that I said just sort of gave us a momentary feeling that maybe life would go on."

In this short anecdote, Davidson brought up three extremely important points about humor and grief.

First, the humor that naturally occurs during times of grief does not have to be prolonged. The briefest of incidents, as Davidson discovered, can be beneficial.

Second, in spite of humor, grief goes on. A humorous encounter, after all, is only a momentary incident—it cannot, and probably should not, substitute for experiencing the grief. Yet in spite of its brevity, it is a very important moment.

And third, as exemplified by Davidson's final comment, no matter how brief, humor can give a sense of hope, which provides us with a powerful message that in spite of the loss, all is *not* lost. Life can and does go on.

> The longer we dwell on our misfortunes, the greater is their power to harm us.
>
> —VOLTAIRE

INNER WISDOM

A number of studies have shown that grief can lower the immune system and leave the body vulnerable to illness. One documented that the lymphocyte response of men who have lost their wives had a significant decline within a month or two of death. Another study found that two common aspects of grief, depression and helplessness, can negatively affect the immune system.

Conversely, the most current research on the benefits of laughter show that it helps boost the immune system. One researcher, Lee Berk, M.D., from Loma Linda University, in California, has shown that cortisol, an immune suppressor, is less prevalent in the blood system when we are laughing, while other immune boosters are more prevalent when we laugh.

On some level, I believe, we instinctively know how valuable humor can be when we get overwhelmed with grief. As Davidson, for example, reports, "I didn't know what to say to my brother—*and then it just came out.*"

Somehow we know that grief is not healthy for us and that humor is. In his book *An Anatomy of Humor,* author Arthur Asa Berger writes that "without being aware of what humor is doing to us and for us, we search it out to deal with needs that we often don't even know we have."

THE SALESMEN GOETH

After my father-in-law died, my mother-in-law kept getting telephone calls from salespeople for her deceased husband. Finally she figured out a way of stopping them from calling back.

When they asked for him, she would say, "He's not here."

"Well then," they would usually ask, "where can I reach him?"

My mother-in-law would reply, "If you want to find him, you'll have to go to hell!"

Then, without saying anything, the caller would abruptly hang up.

Ann Weeks, D.N.S., had a similar experience with people calling to speak to her first husband, who was deceased. She writes about it in her book *She Laughs and the World Laughs with Her:*

> One evening, a couple of months after Paul's death the phone rang. "Hello, Kleine-Kracht's residence," I stated.
>
> "May I speak to Paul Kleine-Kracht?" he said. I caught my breath and said, "I'm sorry Paul is deceased. I'm his wife, may I help you?"
>
> Without any comment about what I'd just said, the caller jumped right in with, "I'm John Jones with the Appliance Warranty Center. I'm calling to remind you that your warranty on your appliance is about to expire and you need to renew it."
>
> "Thank you for calling, but that appliance is several years old and I've decided not to renew the warranty."
>
> With a tone of impatience, he responded, "Well, I'm sure your dead husband would want you to renew."
>
> My humor and coping clicked in as I replied, "Funny you should mention it, but just hours before Paul died he said, 'Honey, whatever you do, don't renew the appliance warranty!'"
>
> There was silence and then Mr. Jones said, "Oh, oh okay," and hung up.

Laughter and tears are both responses to frustration and exhaustion. . . . I myself prefer to laugh, since there is less cleaning up to do afterward.

—KURT VONNEGUT

LAUGHING THRU TEARS

Dacher Keltner, from the University of California, Berkeley, and George Bonanno, from the Catholic University of America, are both researchers investigating laughter in conjunction with bereavement. One of their studies involved thirty-nine people who lost a spouse with whom they had lived with for at least three years. Keltner and Bonanno interviewed these people approximately five months after the death and then again at various intervals. What they found is unique because it goes against the traditional working-through-it approach to grief.

Keltner and Bonanno discovered that authentic laughter and smiling can be beneficial in the grief process because they help the bereaved get through the grief rather than get stuck in it. "The more the bereaved can minimize their emotion when they are talking to someone else," Bonanno said, "and the less they express the negative emotion—the better off they are."

Laughter, Keltner and Bonanno note, switches the bereaved away from pain and helps them dissociate from the distressing emotion associated with loss. Whereas working through grief often focuses on negative feelings, and can therefore interfere with getting on with life, laughter releases the chains that grief may have on the bereaved so that they can move on.

A second thing Keltner and Bonanno have discovered about laughter and grief is that laughter helps enhance social relations after a loss. It therefore can play an important part in readjustment.

Those who were able to laugh and smile about their loss had better social relations and evoked a much more positive response from other people. Those who didn't laugh evoked frustrations and negative emotions from others. In other words, a continued public display of grief was not advantageous.

Bonanno says that "there is probably some private grief people go through but socially, when they are with another person, it is very important to be able to uphold the bounds of a normal social interchange." He concludes, "We are finding pretty clearly that positive emotions really help in bereavement—and laughter in particular."

PLAYING THRU TEARS

Although not a primary mode of treating grief, exaggerated play can be an effective way of easing the tears of the bereaved. In her unpublished thesis on the subject, Betty Blue suggests that by exaggerating their plight the bereaved might begin to see the absurdity of their prolonged sorrow. Humorous play, she says, can help the bereaved get over the emotional ties with the deceased.

An example of this was shared with me by Michael Tarpinian, a young man with AIDS. He said, "I can remember when my lover died. I got a lot of teasing about being a widow. So I went out and bought a big black hat with a big black veil.

"It was a very difficult time for me. I was quite devastated. I couldn't decide if being called a widow was amusing or not. But I decided I had to do something about this—I had to," says Tarpinian. "So I went out and bought this hat and put it on and looked at myself in the mirror so that I could get a sense of this image."

Tarpinian says, "There was something funny about the image that helped me get through that period. I didn't have to feel trapped in my depression. I didn't have to take myself seriously and get caught up in the downside of it all."

In light of studies that show that prolonged grief can be both mentally and physically detrimental, exaggerated play can be a powerful tool to break the stagnation that prevents the survivor from embracing life again.

LEARNING TO LAUGH AGAIN

Can laughter and play really help someone deal with grief, even the grief of losing a young child? According to Lorrie Boyd, a doctor of clinical hypnotherapy, it can. In *Change Your Life with Humor*, which Boyd cowrote, she talks about the death of her son and how important humor, among other things, was for her:

> Jared was in and out of the hospital numerous times. The surgeries, treatments, medications, and other procedures which he had to endure were hard on us and harder on him. Jared's struggle ended Thursday, April 17, 1986 at 10:35 PM.
>
> Instead of dwelling on the many challenges and difficult times we faced with Jared, we focused on all the wonderful things which we had been able to do together. . . .
>
> The other thing that helped me through the grief process was my ability to somehow find humor and joy, and to laugh. I found that every time I laughed, I felt better. So I began seeking out things that would bring me pleasure. Since I had enjoyed *I Love Lucy* so much as a child, I started watching the show again—sometimes once or twice a day. It would make me laugh, and I would feel better. . . .
>
> In summary, our grieving has been a process. It is like a river, and sometimes we get caught up in an eddy, swirling around and around. When this happens, we need the support of others. They help us and we help them. Sometimes we let the current take us down the river of life; at other times, we fight it the entire way.

When we fight the pains of grief, we become exhausted and depleted. However, when we flow with it, we can begin to relax and see the beauty of the shores and the other miracles around us. . . .

In looking back, what helped Chris and me in our grieving was: (1) learning about the grief process itself, (2) having a support system (friends and family), (3) expressing our feelings by talking, writing, and drawing, (4) creating rituals (e.g., sending Jared a balloon on his birthday), and (5) learning to laugh and play again.

TWO ANSWERS TO ONE PRAYER

Steve Wilson is, like myself, a presenter of humor programs. When I interviewed him, Wilson told me about an incident that happened to him related to humor and grief.

"I had always gone out," he said, "to talk to community groups about standard psychological subjects—like marriage, divorce, raising kids, stress, depression, and things like that. One day," Wilson continues, "I get a call from a woman at a cancer clinic who runs a group called Make Today Count. She heard that I give talks and asked that I come and address the group.

"I told her that I had a new talk on humor. She said, 'That would be wonderful. I think the group would really like that.' "

Wilson was excited to do it. His mother had died of ovarian cancer when he was twenty years old, so he thought it would be great if he could be of some help to these people.

There were about thirty-five people seated in a circle that night. To get the meeting started, each person told the group their name, the kind of cancer they had, and the stage of treatment they were in.

The first person said, "My name is Susan. I have a brain tumor. They were able to do surgery and now I'm getting radiation." Then Susan's parents introduced themselves. After that, a young man who was also there with his parents announced that he had lymphoma.

"I started to realize," Wilson admits, "the gravity of the situation these people were in—and there was a room full of them." As each person went around the room, Wilson started to feel inadequate and questioned whether it was right to discuss humor under such circumstances. "Here were people with really catastrophic illnesses in their lives. I worried that my program wasn't appropriate."

To ease his fears, Wilson said a prayer: "God, if this is where you want me to be and there is something in this message that you want these people to hear, then I hope this is the right thing and that you will help me in what I say."

"The prayer was answered in two ways," says Wilson.

First, a man who was introducing himself to the group said, "My name is Lester and I'm pissed off. I have cancer of the liver. My doctor told me I had six months to live. That was a year ago—and I gave away my winter coat."

When everyone in the group started to laugh, it was a validation for Wilson that the group wanted to laugh and that a person in a serious situation could indeed poke fun at himself.

With the knowledge that humor was indeed appropriate, Wilson started his talk. He told jokes, played with props, and explained the value of humor. It was going well. The crowd was laughing loudly and really appreciating what Wilson was doing.

Then there was a knock on the door. A woman opened it and stuck her head in the room. She said, "Listen, I'm trying to run a support group in the room next door"—Wilson thought to himself, "Okay, now I'm in trouble," but the woman continued—"and my group would like to come in and join your group."

It wasn't until after the program that Wilson found out that the second gathering was a support group for those who had recently lost a loved one.

This was the second answer to his prayer. "People who came together to support each other in their grief," says Wilson, "wanted to be where the laughter was."

Mirthful Memories

By their merry talk they cause sufferers to forget grief.

—THE TALMUD

Denying grief is not healthy, but neither is getting stuck in it. Appropriate laughter and humor, on the other hand, can provide a welcomed balance in times of sorrow. Discovering a few funny moments in the midst of loss is not mocking the dead. It is honoring their memory.

In her book *Simple Encounters: Stories of Life, Laughter, and Livelihood,* author and professional speaker Chris Clarke-Epstein writes about remembering the deceased:

> Recently I had the occasion to give a speech that touched on the notion of immortality. It didn't start out to be about that—just a few words to bridge a gap during an after-dinner program.
>
> The founder of the organization's father had died just before the conference and she wanted to say something about him because many in the group knew their family well. Since the focus of the evening was their awards presentation, they asked me to make the transition. As I prepared, I searched for a way to tie the death of a loved one to the recognition of a valued colleague.
>
> What struck me was how we carry little pieces of each other—memories of a precious moment—a piece of knowledge, maybe unknowingly shared.
>
> I remember hearing the words come out of my mouth, "Maybe that's what immortality is—the little pieces of another that we carry in our hearts and minds, pass on to others creating a chain that lasts forever as long as we are active participants in life."

Clarke-Epstein has defined immortality in a simple yet profound way. We can add to her observation, as evidenced in this chapter, that those "pieces of another" frequently revolve around the lighter moments and recollected laughter.

It has been four weeks and it is still hard for me to believe Sandor Needleman is dead. I was present at the cremation and at his son's request, brought the marshmallows, but few of us could think of anything but our pain.

Needleman was constantly obsessing over his funeral plans and once told me, "I much prefer cremation to burial in the earth, and both to a weekend with Mrs. Needleman." In the end, he chose to have himself cremated and donated his ashes to the University of Heidelberg, which scattered them to the four winds and got a deposit on the urn.

—WOODY ALLEN, *Remembering Needleman*

REMEMBERING A LOVABLE ROGUE

During grief, humor often comes in remembering the challenging and absurd times shared between the survivor and the deceased. For example, in *A Laughing Place,* Christian Hageseth writes about a memory of a buddy of his and how laughter helped ease the loss:

> Growing up, I had a best friend. Throughout high school and college I treasured his friendship above all others. While I was on a camping trip in the mountains, he died in a tragic auto accident. No word made it to my wilderness location. I returned home to learn of his death and his funeral which had occurred weeks earlier. We were truly "best friends." I didn't know death could hurt so deeply. I didn't know I had so many tears in my body. I thought I might dehydrate from my crying. Then his mother called me and asked me to drop over to the house and talk to her about some of "those crazy things" Johnny and I did as teenagers. I went to her house. . . . We sat down with coffee and after some more tears, I began to tell some stories she never heard.
>
> Once Johnny and I had been out on the plains driving her big Buick Roadmaster around when we ran out of gas. A helpful farmer allowed us to buy some of his fuel. . . . Unfortunately the fuel wasn't gasoline at all, it was kerosene. The car coughed and sputtered; it worked like a diesel, you couldn't turn it off if you tried. We took the key out and it just chugged and coughed but refused to stop running. We drove directly home, car lurching all the way, and parked it in their garage . . . and went downtown for the rest of the afternoon. When Johnny and I returned to his home that evening, his mother asked what was wrong with the Buick. "The Buick?" we asked incredulously. Why we had no idea, we had been downtown all day. . . .
>
> When I told her the story, we laughed and laughed. We remembered this wonderful, lovable rogue who was gentle and playful and mischievous all in one. In our laughter we remembered our love for him. In our shared laughter we expressed our grief with deep, healing honesty.

REMEMBERING IRENE

Tom Johnson, a sales trainer in northern California, told me that all his life, his aunt Irene was late. She was notorious for never getting anywhere on time. In fact, Johnson says, "we used to tell her that things started an hour or two earlier than they actually did just to get her somewhere on time. But, bless her heart," says Johnson, "she caught on and was late anyway."

Aunt Irene died in New Mexico but was to be buried in Iowa with the rest of her family. Everything was arranged at the graveside—the grave was dug, the mourners were there, the minister was there for the eulogy. "Sure enough, at eleven o'clock that morning," Johnson says, "Aunt Irene's body had not shown up for the funeral." He called the casket people in New Mexico and they didn't know what happened. They could not locate the body, but they said they would.

Aunt Irene eventually did arrive—the next day, on another plane. Johnson recalls, "We all had a laugh that day at the graveside. Aunt Irene was even late for her own funeral!"

REMEMBERING STEPHEN

Stephen was a handsome man who was kind and generous, loving and creative. He was also opinionated and overbearing. Sometimes, in fact, he had to be told to back off so as not to overwhelm people.

Stephen lived in my home for several years. During that time, he told me that the front of the house needed more greenery. The previous owner had stripped off all the Victorian gingerbread and replaced it with ugly pink asbestos shingles. As a professional landscape architect, Stephen suggested that we plant a rapidly growing trumpet vine that would cover up the shingles. We did, and it did.

By the time Stephen had moved out, a couple of years later, the vine not only covered the house but was threatening to take over the entire neighborhood. Every spring it produced hundreds of wonderful, large, bright orange-and-yellow flowers. Tourists and locals alike would stop and take pictures. But as beautiful as the vine was, it took frequent trimming to keep it from blocking all the windows and entryways of the house, as well as climbing the electric wires crossing the street.

The vine continued to grow vigorously, but Stephen did not. He died several years ago. At his memorial service, those who knew him best laughed loudest when I compared Stephen to the trumpet vine—giving of its beauty and strength, yet all too often needing to be trimmed and cut back lest it overwhelm us.

There is a story of an old Taoist scholar who lost his dearly beloved wife. His friends and relatives came to mourn with him, but they found him sitting on the floor and beating a drum singing.

"How can you do this?" his friends demanded. "After all of the years you spent with her, how can you be cheerful at her death?"

"I do love my wife," replied the Taoist. "And when she died I despaired because she was gone. But then I began to think and realized that this is what life is. After all, if I had died first, she would have had to remarry, perhaps someone she did not love, and our children would have been hungry and abused.

"Tears will not change the way life is. My wife is now at peace. If I were to make a lot of noise weeping and wailing, I would disturb her rest. It would show that I know nothing of the ways of life and death."

—BARBARA AND GENE STANFORD, *Myths and Modern Man*

RIBBONS DOWN MY BACK

Rosita Perez creates a striking picture when she is on the speaking platform. She wears wonderful bright-colored dresses that flow across the stage as she moves. She also wears flowers in her hair.

It wasn't until recently that I learned why she wears those flowers. She does so to honor her mother, who died many years ago. "I was so sad when she died," Rosita proclaims; "I was so depressed." Then one day Rosita put a flower behind her ear and she says it transformed her life. "In so doing," she notes, "I remember looking in the mirror and saying, 'Oh, Mama, for the rest of my life I'm going to wear flowers to celebrate the fact that you lived instead of going through life lamenting the fact that you died.' "

One day, after Rosita told that story to her audience, a woman came up to her and said, "Rosita, I didn't realize until this moment why it is I wear ribbons in my hair. I had a little girl," the woman said, "and she died when she was very, very little. I never got a chance to put ribbons in my daughter's hair. I now know why I put them in my own. To celebrate my daughter's life."

PIECES OF ANOTHER

"Laughter when remembering special moments in the life of the deceased," says William F. Fry Jr., M.D., "sets a foundation for cherishing warmth that eases the pain of loss and reunites deceased and bereaved in mirthful memory." Fry also reminds us that these mirthful memories are available whenever we want or need them.

Remembering the laughter of a loved one or "a happy time when . . ." assures us that those who died will lovingly live forever in our minds and our hearts.

Final Words

> The first and last word belong to God and therefore not to death but life, not to sorrow but joy, not to weeping but laughter. For surely, it is God who has the last laugh.
>
> —CONRAD HYERS

SEVERAL years before my father died, I sat down with my parents and recorded an oral history of their growing up. A surprising thing came out of the session.

My mother told me that she did not think that our last name was really *Klein*. Then she explained that my grandparents came from Europe and could speak only Yiddish. When they arrived at Ellis Island, my mother surmises, their Hebrew name was probably changed because the immigration inspectors could not pronounce it. She concluded that since my grandfather was of small stature, they named him *Klein,* which means "little" in German.

As much as I resisted admitting it, my mother was likely right. It was, after all, in keeping with what my father had told me. His first name had been arbitrarily changed when he entered grade school. His Hebrew name, *Naftali,* disappeared, and instantly, from that day onward, my father became *Daniel.*

So my father, Daniel Klein, was buried on January 9, 1997. Or was he? After all, *Daniel* was really *Naftali,* and *Klein* was—well, who knows what?

When I thought about my father's name change, I also remembered a custom in the Hasidic Jewish tradition. When a child becomes seriously ill, its name is changed so that the Angel of Death cannot find them.

In reality, of course, you can't really escape the Angel of Death. Death always finds you. Sometimes it takes a while, but Death is very persistent. My father had a different name all his life, and Death finally found him.

But there is more to this name story . . .

At one moment during the memorial service at my father's graveside, the rabbi mistakenly referred to my father as *Daniel Levine.* Amid the snickers from the crowd, I chuckled. "Ah, finally," I thought, "I now know my true last name."

Then another bizarre incident occurred. Two days later, while still sitting shivah, I was glancing at an article in a magazine. The author? You guessed it—Daniel Levine!

So what is the point to this closing story? The point is that there is always something to chuckle about. Sometimes we see it. Sometimes, especially when we are dealing with death or grief, we don't. Still, the world is filled with humor. It is there when we are happy and it is there to cheer us up when we are not.

Celebrate the tears.

Celebrate the laughter.

Permissions

Excerpt from "Cancer Becomes Me" by Marjorie Gross used by permission of the author. Originally published in *The New Yorker.*

Excerpt from "Cancer Is a Funny Thing" by J. B. S. Haldane originally published in the *New Statesman,* 1964. Reprinted by permission of the Guardian & Observer News Services.

"Doctors Are Whippersnappers" by Gilda Radner, from *The New England Journal of Medicine,* vol. 319, p. 1358. Reprinted by permission. Copyright © 1988 Massachusetts Medical Society. All rights reserved.

Excerpts from *First, You Cry* by Betty Rollins, copyright © 1976. Reprinted by permission of HarperCollins Publishers.

Excerpts from *Flying Without Wings* by Arnold Beisser. Copyright © 1989 by Arnold Beisser. Used by permission of Doubleday, a division of Bantam Doubleday Dell Publishing Group, Inc.

Excerpt from "Forest Lawn" by Tom Paxton. Copyright © 1969 (Renewed) EMI U Catalog Inc. All rights reserved. Used by permission of Warner Bros. Publications U.S. Inc.

Excerpts from *How Am I Gonna Find a Man If I'm Dead?* by Fanny Gaynes, copyright © 1994. Reprinted by permission of Morgin Press, Inc.

Excerpts from Howard Shapiro's "Kvetch" columns reprinted with permission from *Body Positive,* Inc. © 1997. All rights reserved.

"Resume" by Dorothy Parker, copyright 1926, 1928, renewed 1954, © 1956 by Dorothy Parker. "Tombstones in the Starlight" by Dorothy Parker, copyright 1928, renewed © 1956 by Dorothy Parker, from *The Portable Dorothy Parker* by Dorothy Parker. Introduction by Brendan Gill. Used by permission of Viking Penguin, a division of Penguin Books USA Inc.

Excerpts from "Virginia's Last Request" by Hanna-Ian Faraclas used by permission of the author. Originally published by Global City Press in *The Breast: An Anthology* by Susan Thames and Marin Gazzaniga.

Bibliography

THERE is little written about humor in the death, dying, and grieving process. To my knowledge, this is the first book to focus entirely on this subject. There are, however, a handful of articles that deal with humor and death, as well as books that contain a related story or two. The items below generally fall into those categories.

Adams, Patch, and Maureen Mylander. *Gesundheit!* Rochester, VT: Healing Arts Press, 1993.

Allen, Steve, Jr. "Healing in the 90's: If I Didn't Laugh, I'd Cry." Speech presented at the Anderson Cancer Network Conference, Houston, TX, 1995.

Beisser, Arnold. *Flying Without Wings.* New York: Doubleday, 1989.

Blue, Betty. "Humorous Play: A Transcendent Approach Toward Unresolved Grief." Dissertation, California Graduate Institute, 1981.

Bombeck, Erma. *I Want to Grow Hair, I Want to Grow Up, I Want to Go to Boise: Children Surviving Cancer.* New York: Harper & Row, 1989.

Bonanno, George. "The Concept of 'Working Through' Loss." In *Posttraumatic Stress Disorder,* edited by A. Maercker and M. Schuetzwohl. Seattle: Hogrefe and Huber, in press.

Bonham, Tal. *Humor: God's Gift.* Nashville: Broadman Press, 1988.

Boorstein, Sylvia. *It's Easier Than You Think.* New York: HarperCollins, 1995.

Boyd, Lorrie, Lola Gillebaard, and Stewart and Jeanne Lerner. *Change Your Life with Humor.* Brea, CA: Lerner and Associates, 1993.

Brown, Mark. *Emergency!: True Stories from the Nation's ERs.* New York: Villard Books, 1996.

Broyard, Anatole. *Intoxicated by My Illness.* New York: Fawcett Columbine, 1992.

Buchanan, Sue. *Love, Laughter and a High Disregard for Statistics.* Nashville, TN: Thomas Nelson, 1994.

Buckley, J. Taylor. "Telling Tombstones." *USA Today,* February 13, 1996, 1A–2A.

Buxman, Karyn, and Anne LeMoine, eds. *Nursing Perspectives on Humor.* New York: Power Publications, 1995.

Callahan, John. *Don't Worry He Won't Get Far on Foot.* New York: William Morrow, 1989.

Callen, Michael. *Surviving AIDS.* New York: HarperCollins, 1990.

Canfield, Jack, et al. *Chicken Soup for the Surviving Soul.* Deerfield Beach, FL: Health Communications, 1996.

Carroll, Jon. "Nothing Is Not Funny." *San Francisco Chronicle,* August 8, 1997, D16.

———. "Good Times During Bad Times." *San Francisco Chronicle,* August 15, 1997, C18.

Center for Attitudinal Healing. *There Is a Rainbow Behind Every Dark Cloud.* Berkeley, CA: Celestial Arts, 1978.

———. *Advice to Doctors and Other Big People . . . from Kids.* Berkeley, CA: Celestial Arts, 1991.

Chandler, Marilyn. "Healthy Irreverence: Humor in Stories of Illness." *International Journal of Humor Research* 1, no. 3 (1988): 299–305.

Cicero, Christina. "The Treatment of Death and Dying in the Television Program 'Northern Exposure.' " Thesis, University of Oklahoma, Graduate College, Norman, OK, 1993.

Clarke-Epstein, Chris. *Simple Encounters.* Wausau, WI: Another Pair of Shoes Press, 1995.

Clifford, Christine. *Not Now . . . I'm Having a No Hair Day.* Duluth, MN: Pfeifer-Hamilton, 1996.

Corpany, Susan. *Unfinished Business.* Edmonton, Alta.: Commonwealth Publications, 1997.

Cousins, Norman. *Anatomy of an Illness.* New York: W. W. Norton, 1979.

———. *Head First: The Biology of Hope.* New York: E. P. Dutton, 1989.

Darrach, Brad. "Send in the Clowns." *Life,* August 1990, 77–85.

de Solla Price, Mark. *Living Positively in a World with HIV/AIDS.* New York: Avon Books, 1995.

DeSpelder, Lynne Ann, and Albert Lee Strickland. *The Last Dance.* Mountain View, CA: Mayfield, 1996.

Dundes, Alan. *Cracking Jokes.* Berkeley, CA: Ten Speed Press, 1987.

Dunn, Joseph. "Humor, Health, and Dying—An Interview with Allen Klein." *Humor and Health Letter* 2, no. 6 (1993): 1–4.

Eckardt, A. Roy. *On the Way to Death.* New Brunswick, NJ: Transaction Publishers, 1996.

———. *Sitting in the Earth and Laughing.* New Brunswick, NJ: Transaction Publishers, 1992.

Eliach, Yaffa. *Hasidic Tales of the Holocaust.* New York: Oxford University Press, 1982.

Erdman, Lynn. "Laughter Therapy for Patients with Cancer." *Oncology Nursing Forum* 18, no. 8 (1991): 1359–63.

Faraclas, Hanna-Ian. "The Healthy Breast." In *The Breast: An Anthology,* edited by Susan Thames and Marin Gazzaniga. New York: Global City Press, 1995.

Felder, Leonard. *When a Loved One Is Ill.* New York: NAL Books, 1990.

Finnerty, Amy. "Send in the Clowns." *American Health,* September 1995, 68–69, 105.

Fox, Renee. *Experiment Perilous.* Glencoe, IL: The Free Press, 1959.

Frankl, Viktor. *Man's Search for Meaning.* New York: Simon & Schuster, 1963.

Fulghum, Robert. *Uh-Oh.* New York: Villard Books, 1991.

———. "Lessons from the Sandbox." Speech presented at the National Hospice Organization Conference, Detroit, MI, November 1990.

Gaes, Jason. *My Book for Kids with Cansur.* Aberdeen, SD: Melius & Peterson, 1987.

Gaynes, Fanny. *How Am I Gonna Find a Man If I'm Dead?* Wayne, PA: Morgin Press, 1994.

Goodheart, Annette. *Laughter Therapy.* Santa Barbara, CA: Less Stress Press, 1994.

Gordon, Sol, and Harold Brecher. *Life Is Uncertain . . . Eat Dessert First!* New York: Delacorte Press, 1990.

Gravy, Wavy. *Something Good for a Change.* New York: St. Martin's Press, 1992.

Grollman, Earl. *When Your Loved One Is Dying.* Boston: Beacon Press, 1980.

Gross, Marjorie. "Cancer Becomes Me." *New Yorker,* April 15, 1996, 54–55.

Hageseth, Christian. *A Laughing Place.* Fort Collins, CO: Berwick, 1988.

Hall, Mary, and Paula Rappe. "Humor and Critical Incident Stress." In *The Path Ahead: Readings in Death and Dying,* edited by Lynne Ann DeSpelder and Albert Lee Strickland, 289–94. Mountain View, CA: Mayfield, 1995.

Hammerschlag, Carl. *The Theft of the Spirit.* New York: Simon & Schuster, 1992.

Hart, Judy. *Love, Judy.* Berkeley, CA: Conari Press, 1993.

Henry, Janet. *Surviving the Cure!: " . . . A Time to Laugh."* Cleveland, OH: Cope, 1984.

Herth, Kaye Ann. "Humor's Role in Terminal Illness." In *Nursing Perspective on Humor,* edited by K. Buxman and A. LeMoine, 217–30. New York: Power Publications, 1995.

———. "Contributions of Humor As Perceived by the Terminally Ill." *American Journal of Hospice Care* 7, no. 1 (1990): 36–40.

Hitchens, Neal. *Voices That Care.* Los Angeles: Lowell House, 1992.

Hoffman, Deborah. *Complaints of a Dutiful Daughter.* Women Make Movies, New York: 1994. Documentary film.

Hughes, Phyllis Rash. "Guest Editor Explores Some Unique Ways of Coping with Grief." *The Forum: Newsletter of the Association for Death Education and Counseling* 5, no. 10 (1981): 1–2.

Jenkins, Ron. *Subversive Laughter.* New York: The Free Press, 1994.

Jevne, Ronna Fay. *It All Begins with Hope.* San Diego, Calif.: LuraMedia, 1991.

Jevne, Ronna Fay, and Alexander Levitan. *No Time for Nonsense.* San Diego, Calif.: LuraMedia, 1989.

Johnston, Wayne. "To the Ones Left Behind." *American Journal of Nursing,* August 1985, 936.

Keelan, Jim. *Laugh Your Way to Health.* Arvada, Colo.: Communication Unlimited, n.d.

Keltner, Dacher, and George Bonanno. "A Study of Laughter and Dissociation." *Journal of Personal and Social Psychology,* under review.

Kershner, Kelly McConaghy. "Comedy and Cancer." *Frontiers,* autumn 1996, 20–23, 28.

Kisner, Bette. "The Use of Humor in Treatment of People with Cancer." In *The Handbook of Humor,* edited by Elcha Shain Buckman. Malabar, FL: Krieger, 1994.

Klein, Allen. "Did You Die Today?" *Prevention,* March 1981, 95–99.

———. *The Healing Power of Humor.* New York: Tarcher/Putnam, 1989.

———. "Humor and Death: You've Got to be Kidding." *American Journal of Hospice Care* 3, no. 4 (1986): 42–45.

———. "Last Laugh." *Hospice,* summer 1994, 8–9.

————. *Quotations to Cheer You Up When the World is Getting You Down.* New York: Wings Books/Random House, 1991.

Kuhlman, Thomas. *Humor and Psychotherapy.* Homewood, IL: Dow Jones–Irwin, 1984.

Kuhn, Clifford. "Laughing Through Tears—Humor as a Resource in Grief." Speech presented at the Humor Skills for the Health Professional Conference, St. Louis, MO: June 1996.

Lipman, Steve. *Laughter in Hell: The Use of Humor During the Holocaust.* Northvale, NJ: Jason Aronson, 1991.

Litman, Robert. "Grave Humor." In *A Celebration of Laughter,* edited by Werner Mendel. Los Angeles: Mara Books, 1970.

London, Oscar. *Kill as Few Patients as Possible.* Berkeley, CA: Ten Speed Press, 1987.

Madden, Ed. *Carpe Diem: Enjoying Every Day with a Terminal Illness.* Boston: Jones and Barlett, 1993.

McGrann, John, ed. "Cultivating Humor: An Interview with Danny Williams." *Kairos News* (San Francisco) 4, no. 29 (1993): 1, 4–5.

Metcalf, C. W. "Humor, Life and Death." *Oncology Nursing Forum* 14 (1987): 19–21.

Metcalf, C. W., and Roma Felible. *Lighten Up.* Reading, MA: Addison-Wesley, 1992.

Middlebrook, Christina. *Seeing the Crab: A Memoir of Dying.* New York: Basic Books, 1996.

Mikes, George. *Humour in Memoriam.* London: Routledge & Kegan Paul, 1970.

Mindess, Harvey. *Laughter and Liberation.* Los Angeles: Nash, 1971.

Mitchell, Jim. "Taking It to the Limit: The Role of Humor in Surviving Extreme Situations." *Humor and Health Journal* 5, no. 6 (1996): 1–8.

Moody, Raymond. *Laugh After Laugh.* Jacksonville, FL: Headwaters Press, 1978.

Nelsen, Donna Enoch, *One Life to Laugh.* Glendale, CA: Potentials, 1990.

Nisker, Wes "Scoop." *Crazy Wisdom.* Berkeley, CA: Ten Speed Press, 1990.

Novak, William, and Moshe Waldoks, eds. "First Things Last." In *The Big Book of Jewish Humor,* 292–305. New York: Harper & Row, 1981.

O'Connell, Walter. "Humor and Death." *Psychological Reports* 22 (1968): 391–402.

Pitzele, Sefra Kobrin. *We Are Not Alone.* New York: Workman, 1986.

Remen, Rachel Naomi. *Kitchen Table Wisdom.* New York: Riverhead Books, 1996.

Rivers, Joan, and Richard Merryman. *Still Talking.* New York: Random House, 1991.

Ritz, Sandra. "Disaster Relief." *Laugh It Up* 7, no. 4: 1–2.

Robinson, Vera. *Humor and the Health Professions.* Thorofare, NJ: Charles B. Slack, 1977.

Rollin, Betty. *First, You Cry.* Philadelphia, PA: Lippincott, 1976.

Rosenberg, Lisa. "A Qualitative Investigation of the Use of Humor by Emergency Personnel as a Strategy for Coping with Stress." *Journal of Emergency Nursing* 17 (1991): 197–203.

Sacks, Oliver. *A Leg to Stand On.* New York: Harper & Row, 1984.

Seligson, Ross, and Karen Peterson. *AIDS Prevention and Treatment: Hope, Humor, and Healing.* New York: Hemisphere, 1992.

Serchia, Paul. Articles in *Positive Living* (Los Angeles AIDS Project), February 1993–November 1996.

Shapiro, Howard. Articles in *The Body Positive* (New York), June 1993–July 1996.

Shephard, Martin. *Someone You Love Is Dying.* New York: Charter, 1975.

Showalter, Sherry, and Steven Skobel. "Hospice: Humor, Heartache and Healing." *American Journal of Hospice and Palliative Care* 13 (1996): 8–9.

Siegel, Bernie. *How to Live Between Office Visits.* New York: HarperCollins, 1993.

———. *Love, Medicine, and Miracles.* New York: Harper & Row, 1986.

Snead, Elizabeth. "Death Is Becoming Less of a Grave Subject." *USA Today,* January 8, 1992.

Solomon, Phyllis Schwied. "Humor Appreciation and Coping with Dying Patients." Master's dissertation, California State University, Dominquez Hills, CA., 1981.

Stacy, Barbara. "Helping Kids Cope with Terminal Illness." *East West,* July 1987, 37–41.

Stanford, Barbara, with Gene Stanford. *Myths and Modern Man.* New York: Pocket Books, 1972.

Summers, Caryn. *Inspirations for Caregivers.* Mount Shasta, CA: Commune-A-Key, 1993.

Sweeney, Julia. *God Said, "Ha!"* New York: Bantam Doubleday Dell, 1997.

Thompson, Barbara Adams. *Sometimes We Laughed.* Glastonbury, CT: Star Press, 1995.

Thorson, James. "A Funny Thing Happened on the Way to the Morgue." *Death Studies* 9 (1985): 201–16.

Torbet, Laura. "Last Laughs at the Last Suppers." *Living/Dying Project Newsletter*, winter 1996, n.p.

Vernon, Glenn. *Sociology of Death.* New York: Ronald Press, 1970.

Weeks, Ann. *She Laughs and the World Laughs with Her.* Louisville, KY: Passages, 1995.

Whipple, Barbara. *I've Got Cancer, but It Doesn't Have Me!* Westmont, IL: Full Moon Press, 1995.

Wilber, Ken. *Grace and Grit.* Boston: Shambhala Publications, 1991.

Wooten, Patty. *Compassionate Laughter.* Salt Lake City, UT: Commune-a-Key, 1996.

———. *Heart, Humor and Healing.* Salt Lake City, UT: Commune-a-Key, 1994.

Yacowar, Maurice. *Loser Take All: The Comic Art of Woody Allen.* New York: Frederick Ungar, 1979.

Zimmerman, David. " 'Doonesbury' Laughs in the Face of AIDS." *USA Today*, April 10, 1989.

Also available from Jeremy P. Tarcher/Putnam
by Allen Klein

The Healing Power of Humor

*Techniques for Getting through Loss, Setbacks, Upsets,
Disappointments, Difficulties, Trials, Tribulations,
and All That Not-So-Funny Stuff*

Foreword by O. Carl Simonton, M.D.

"Provides practical advice as to the fundamental importance of humor and laughter."

—STEVE ALLEN

"A must gift for anyone in the hospital, sick bed, or just feeling blue."

—HAROLD BLOOMFIELD, M.D.,
author of *Making Peace with Yourself*

Brimming with humorous anecdotes, *The Healing Power of Humor* guarantees to help you turn life's negatives into positives. A classic in its field, this book is used in classrooms and is recommended by the health care industry nationwide. ISBN 0-87477-519-1 ★ $11.95 ($16.50 CAN)

This book is available at your local bookstore or wherever books are sold. Ordering is also easy and convenient. To order, call 1-800-788-6262.

About the Author

Allen Klein is an award-winning professional speaker and best-selling author who shows people nationwide how to deal with not-so-funny stuff. Klein is the recipient of a Toastmaster's International Leadership Award and was honored with a Certified Speaking Professional designation from the National Speakers Association. Klein's previous books include *The Healing Power of Humor* (Tarcher/Putnam), *Quotations to Cheer You Up When the World is Getting You Down* (Wings/Random House) and *Wing Tips* (Wings/Random House). For more information about his programs, Allen Klein can be contacted at 1034 Page Street, San Francisco, CA 94117 or at http://www.allenklein.com